The Meditative Gardener

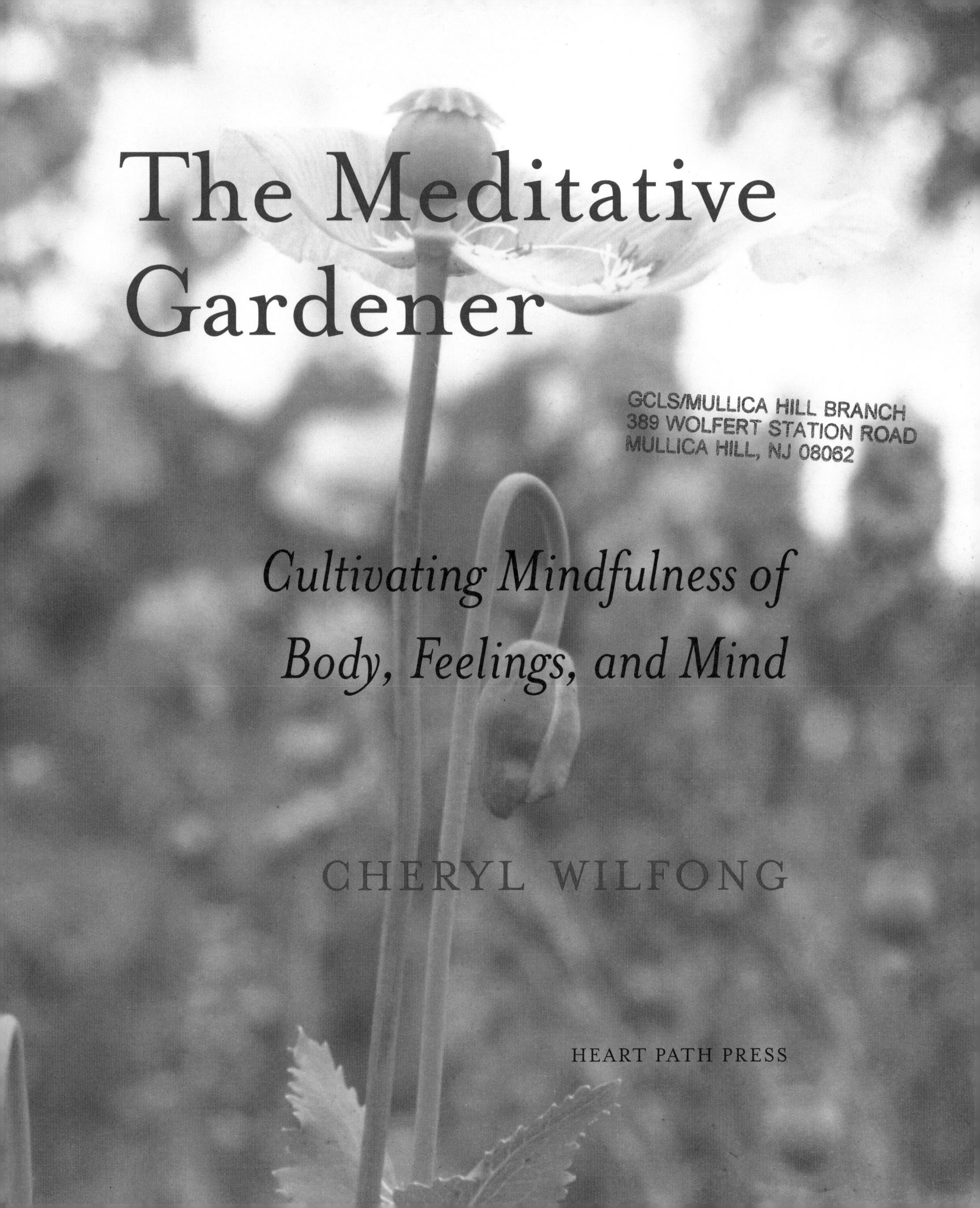

The Meditative Gardener

Cultivating Mindfulness of
Body, Feelings, and Mind

CHERYL WILFONG

HEART PATH PRESS

Cheryl Wilfong
Heart Path Press, L3C
P.O. Box 336
Putney VT 05346
www.meditativegardener.com

First Edition
10 9 8 7 6 5 4 3 2

Photography by Lynne Weinstein and Gene Parulis,
with Lea Carmichael, Rebecca Dixon, and Coni Richards.

Printed in the United States of America

ISBN: 978-0-615-30041-2

Via is made with Green-E certified renewable wind-generated electricity.

Printed on paper with pulp that comes from FSC
(Forest Stewardship Council) certified forests, managed forests that
guarantee responsible environmental, social, and economic practices.
Made with a chlorine-free process (ECF: Elemental Chlorine Free).

BOOK DESIGN BY DEDE CUMMINGS & CAROLYN KASPER
DCDESIGN, BRATTLEBORO, VERMONT

With great gratitude to my teachers

Andrew Olendzki and Gloria Taraniya Ambrosia

Leigh Brasington and,

although I never met her,

Ayya Khema

CONTENTS

FEELINGS

MIND

CONTEMPLATIONS

INTRODUCTION

For years I tried to coax a lush English garden out of the stony, unyielding ground of my New England home. The results were dismal until I made a commitment to improve the soil. Slowly, over a number of years, I added loads of cow, rabbit, and other manures, whatever I could find at nearby farms. The earth grew rich, dark, and alive with wriggling worms, finally yielding the abundant blooms and fruits I sought.

Likewise, I meditated for I-don't-want-to-tell-you-how-long, before my practice began to bear fruit. To begin with, I meditated irregularly—two months of sitting every day followed by a couple of months of not sitting. I occasionally read something on the Buddha's teachings, the Dharma. It was a little like gardening without a guide and without attending to the basics—the soil. You can do it, but really, the chances of success with flowers and meditation improve greatly when you find a teacher or a book whose Wisdom and experience can guide you. Some years ago, while listening to a talk by a meditation teacher, I suddenly realized what I needed to do: weed my inner garden to improve the conditions for the flowering of skillful habits.

It took time to discover the perfect meditation microclimate that fosters the flowering of my love for the Dharma. Meditation doesn't thrive in a busy, weedy Mind, or in a bored, dry Mind. Meditation succeeds when the Mind is happy. My Mind is happy when I'm in the garden. If you're browsing through this book, you're probably happy in the garden as well. My meditation microclimate includes daily sitting practice and reflection on the Dharma. Sitting regularly with a community of meditating friends, called a sangha, is like companion planting—we support each other in our practice. Digging through the Buddha's teachings under the direction of a meditation teacher brings a renewed level of intention and commitment to my meditation practice. Planting Contemplations into my daily meditation gives rise

to insights. This is how I learn best. I sit regularly with my neighbors and we read and discuss a Dharma book; I go on retreat for several weeks each year. That's how my meditation practice flourishes.

Today I teach meditation classes, give Dharma talks, and lead one-day retreats in Brattleboro, Vermont, where I live. I also serve as a consultant to local gardeners. This book is the result of my two passions: meditating and gardening. I love gardening so much that I took a Master Gardener course from the state university extension service. People in my local garden club ask me questions about plants (and soil). I don't know all the answers, but I love to talk gardening, and I've attended enough gardening workshops that neighbors and acquaintances ask my advice about the design of their gardens. In this book I offer you the opportunity to practice meditation and reflect on the Buddha's teachings in the pleasant surroundings of your garden.

Just as we cultivate our flower, vegetable, and herb gardens, we can bring such intention and effort to nurturing our inner garden by paying attention to what are called "the Four Foundations of Mindfulness." They are Body, Feelings, Mind, and Contemplations. These Four Foundations can support our meditation practice as stone, concrete, and cinderblock foundations bear our houses. The Buddha's teachings on the Four Foundations of Mindfulness have been so important to my meditation practice that I want to share them with you. I have based this book of gardening meditations on them.

The Four Foundations offer a broad variety of meditations to enliven our practices and keep our Minds interested and involved. We can build our meditations by focusing on the sensations in our bodies (and by paying attention to our breath); by focusing on whether what we are feeling is pleasant or unpleasant or even neutral; and by becoming of aware of our states of Mind. Finally, we can contemplate the laws of nature while we are amid its beauty.

As gardeners, we have a unique opportunity to observe nature close up. The Buddha's teachings help us understand the similarities between nature and human nature. A key teaching is that everything changes. So, new flowers arise and old ones cease flowering. We are happy when the sights and sounds of the garden delight us; we are sad when the blooming and growing season ends. If we sow peas, we will harvest peas, not beans; these natural consequences indicate the laws of cause and effect of which the Buddha spoke.

How to Use this Book

Many books have been written about creating spiritual gardens, Zen landscapes, and sacred spaces, as if improving our gardens would improve our spiritual lives. While sacred spaces are certainly restful and calming, we are ordinary gardeners with busy lives. We don't need to build a green cathedral in order to find peace of Mind. If we look, we can find the sacred in a single flower. If we pause, we can feel the spiritual in the sanctuary of an ordinary garden. If we practice Mindfulness, we realize we don't have to improve anything; we need only bring awareness to the time we spend in the garden.

So the emphasis of *The Meditative Gardener* is simply on being in the garden that you have. The garden can be relatively quiet; the Mind may calm down a bit and you may just feel plain happy to be where you are. Quiet, Calm, and happy—these are excellent ingredients for practicing Mindfulness.

You don't have to change or *do* anything to your garden. Whether you garden in a flower box or a flower bed or have an extensive garden, whether you meditate daily or never, pick just a few of the suggestions in this book and see what happens. I invite you to dip into the book and select one Contemplation a day, a week, a month.

This is my wish for you, dear reader: May you find something in this book to help you be mindful while you go about your daily life. For mature practitioners, who already meditate regularly, I offer you these Contemplations as a way of refreshing and deepening your practice. I also hope that this book will serve as a field guide in identifying and categorizing some of the Buddha's teachings.

I have recorded the meditations and you can download (and listen to) them at www.meditativegardener.com.

Please write your insights and journal entries right in this book, so that you can review your thoughts in the future. Budding insights can easily get lost in the jungle of daily life; reviewing your insights will help them take root in your life. Alternatively, you may purchase The Meditative Gardener Notebook at www.meditativegardener.com.

So I offer you this book—a collection of meditations, Contemplations, and Investigations, based on the Buddha's teachings, specifically the Four Foundations of Mindfulness. You can take this book out to the garden, which is where I'm going now. A robin calls "Cheer-up. Cheer-ly" as I bend over to smell flowering laven-

der. I am walking, walking. I stop to greet other old flower friends and call them by name: Lily. Petunia. Iris, Geranium. Then I spot a rose that wasn't blooming yesterday.

May you be joyful in your garden.

English or Latin or Pali?

I am a gardener who likes to use Latin names for plants because Latin is so descriptive.[1] *Geranium macrorhizum* (big-root geranium) beautifully describes this all-purpose ground cover.

I also like to use Pali, the language of the Buddha's teachings, which is a language closely related to Sanskrit. Sanskrit words such as Dharma (Pali: *dhamma*) and karma (Pali: *kamma*) have entered the English language, but the Pali word Metta (Sanskrit: *maitri*) which means Goodwill or Loving-Kindness is still a foreigner to most English-speakers.

Although English has a vast vocabulary to describe the material world, I often find Pali words describe the inner world much more precisely. Metta, for example, is much more specific than the English word "love" which covers everything from a flower to your favorite food to your home to your child to your lover.

However, many gardeners stumble over Latin and most meditators are stumped by Pali. To keep us all happy, I will use English words followed by Pali or Sanskrit in parentheses.

Please use the Glossary at the back of this book.

TOOLS *for* MEDITATING IN THE GARDEN

Mindfulness and Goodwill

J ust as we bring trowel, gloves, and clippers with us into the garden, we can also carry some meditation tools. This book offers many such tools, but right now I want to highlight two: Mindfulness and Goodwill.

Mindfulness is the key to our secret garden. When we come to meditation for the first time we are introduced to Mindfulness of the Body through Mindfulness of the breath. As we focus on hearing, touching, smelling, tasting, seeing, we experience Mindfulness of the Body through all our senses. Then we become aware of Mindfulness of the Body in all its positions—sitting, walking, standing, or lying down. Eventually we find out that the Body is just one of the Four Foundations of Mindfulness that includes Mindfulness of Feelings, Mindfulness of the Mind, and Mindfulness of what the Mind is thinking about—Contemplations. We meet Right Mindfulness when we step onto the Noble Eightfold Path. And, as a Factor of Awakening, Mindfulness can wake us up.

We might use the forget-me-not as an emblem of Mindfulness in the garden. These little blue flowers are so exuberant in my garden that they re-seed themselves along the woodchip paths every year. Would that our Mindfulness—our "forget not"—placed itself in our paths to remind us, "Oh, yes. Mindfulness. That's what I'm doing here. I'm walking. I'm bending over."

Goodwill (*Metta*), the second tool, is what is called a Divine Abode—a place where the divine in our heart dwells. Metta is also a quality of goodness, a Perfection. The Buddha first taught Metta to a group of young monks who were afraid to go into the forest by themselves to meditate, as he had instructed. They worried that the tree spirits (and perhaps other wild things) were malevolent, so the Buddha recommended practicing Metta toward all the spirits that resided in the forest, and toward themselves. As they did so, the monks calmed their fears and became happier.

I propose that we first have Goodwill toward our garden. Goodwill toward the very garden that grows outside our home right now. That garden is our refuge, our sanctuary where we meditate and contemplate, and work and play.

One friend really does like to garden, but for years she experienced her garden as a burden. There is so much work to do and she doesn't have time. She likes to do everything right, which means reading up on which manure is the best or which mulch is best, and then trying to find a source for it. She carefully reads about when to plant which vegetable seed. She likes to follow directions; she wants to garden correctly. She also likes to talk things through with her husband and come to an agreement on who does what when.

In the midst of all this doing and organizing for doing, she lost her Goodwill toward her picture-perfect vegetable garden. After taking a long break from gardening for some years, she eventually settled on having a flower bed beside her front door. There. That satisfies her desire to garden, it looks good, and it isn't too much to do. Now she enjoys going out to the garden again.

Having Goodwill toward the garden is important, but even more important is having Goodwill toward the gardener, which is to say, yourself.

The gardener of your garden is doing the best she can, using her time and knowledge to the best of her abilities. She may not get all the weeding done or all the seeds planted or all the plants watered, but she is doing the best she can, under the circumstances. She labors in your garden for the sheer love of it.

Sometimes gardening can be challenging, but we don't go to the garden to be bothered—by people or insects or plants. We go for enjoyment, for the pleasure of being in the garden and maybe to just get away from it all for a little while. If we practice Goodwill toward ourselves as gardeners, our gardens will benefit. Let's begin now with the practice of Goodwill toward our garden and Goodwill toward our gardener, our self.

THE MEDITATIVE GARDENER

A Flower in Your Heart[2]

You love gardens or you would not have picked up this book. You love flowers or vegetables and you love being in a garden. So let's start here, in a place that makes you happy, a place that brings you pleasure and maybe even Calm and peace.

While sitting on a meditation cushion, chair, or garden bench, try this visualization:

Sitting in a comfortable position, with your eyes closed or resting softly on the ground in front of you, feel your breath coming in and going out for a few moments.

Imagine strolling through a garden and choosing the most beautiful flower. Feel its presence in your heart. Invite this blossom to grow in your heart. Let this beautiful flower of love expand, so that you are totally filled with the all-encompassing fragrance of love.

Expand this beautiful flower until it is as large as yourself, filled with the most wonderful aroma. Offer this flower of love to your most beloved person, without expecting anything in return.

Then, hand a flower like that, a flower containing all your love, a flower as large as yourself, with the most delightful aroma, to the people nearest and dearest to you. Watch the flower grow within them until it is large enough to fill each person with love from head to toe, and it is so beautiful that they radiate Joy and delight.

Hand a flower to each of your friends, giving them the gift of love and Goodwill from your heart, in the form of a beautiful flower.

Notice that the flower garden in your heart has become even larger and is now burgeoning with fragrant flowers.

Give a beautiful flower of love to all the people who come into your life; those you've met just briefly, those whom you see often. Offer all of them the gift of a flower from your heart.

Extend a beautiful flower to one person whom you don't particularly like.

Grow as many flowers of love in your heart as possible. Hand those beautiful flowers to as many people as you can think of.

Come back to your own heart and observe the beautiful flowers of love growing and expanding. Cherish and cultivate them. Let the beautiful aroma surround and fill you. Let the feeling of having such beauty within bring happiness and Joy to you.

May all beings have love and Goodwill in their hearts.

GOODWILL OR METTA IS ALSO translated as Loving-Kindness[3] or Loving-Friendliness. Goodwill begins with a basic friendliness toward yourself, like the conventional Wisdom that says, "You can't love someone else if you don't love yourself."

Sometimes that feeling of Goodwill toward yourself can be hard to find, so phrases are said such as:

> May I feel safe.
> May I feel happy.
> May I feel strong.
> May I feel peaceful.
> May I be free from danger.
> May I dwell in the heart.
> May I have mental happiness.
> May I be healed.
> May I be filled with love.
> May I be free from Suffering.
> May I abide in well-being.

Practice by repeating the three or four phrases that feel right for you. Over time you can play with these phrases or graft other words onto them until you find the words that resonate with you.

Even though you may not feel particularly loving or kind, the repetition of these phrases serves to water the seeds of Goodwill and Loving-Kindness. Be patient. Germination can take more than a month of daily sunshine and watering. Then, suddenly, you may notice two tiny new leaves of open-heartedness in a place where you've never seen them before.

The phrases that work for me are

_____

_____

_____

_____

When I was practicing metta intensively in Burma, at times when I repeated the phrases, I would picture myself in a wide-open field planting seeds. Doing metta, we plant the seeds of love, knowing that nature will take its course and in time those seeds will bear fruit. Some seeds will come to fruition quickly, some slowly, but our work is simply to plant the seeds. Every time we form the intention in the Mind for our own happiness or for the happiness of others, we are doing our work; we are channeling the powerful energies of our own Minds. Beyond that, we can trust the laws of nature to continually support the flowering of our love.

Sharon Salzberg

Practicing Goodwill toward Yourself

Begin by directing Goodwill and a feeling of friendliness toward yourself. Whisper the phrases in your Mind even if you do not feel the feeling behind the words. "May I feel safe. May I feel happy. May I feel strong. May I feel peaceful." Use your own phrases.

THE SEED OF ENLIGHTENMENT

T HE SEED OF ENLIGHTENMENT IS already growing in your heart. Meditation practice is the sunshine that warms the soil around that seed. A weekly sitting group nourishes that seed by watering the roots. Meditation books, such as the one you are holding in your hands, fertilize that seed of enlightenment sprouting in your heart of hearts.

You can sow the seeds of your practice directly into the soil at home or attend a meditation retreat, which is a greenhouse in which to grow your meditation practice, but your meditation practice needs to be tended. The fruits of meditation cannot simply be transplanted into your life. Tending the meditation practice starts by planting yourself in the right microclimate at your home and watering the seeds of practice.

Go ahead. Taste the first fruit of enlightenment—Mindfulness of the present moment. Let's go out to the garden.

BODY

THE GARDEN IS OUR REFUGE from the world. In this sanctuary we gardeners are in constant motion—walking, sitting, kneeling, standing, and bending over. Once in a while we may even actually sit down or lie down.

The Buddha described four postures for meditating—sitting, walking, standing, and lying down. Our meditation practice begins with the Body.

Your Body has carried you all your life. When you were younger you may have taken the Body for granted—or maybe you were overly focused on it. Perhaps now, after having suffered an injury, or feeling the first aches and pains of aging, you may feel somewhat less confident about a Body that once seemed indestructible. Yet bodily pain can diminish, if only momentarily, when you are doing an activity that you love, such as gardening; mental Stress decreases in the garden, as well.

Two thousand five hundred years ago, the Buddha instructed his monks and nuns to go to the forest to meditate. Sitting cross-legged at the base of a tree or in an empty hut, the Buddha and his disciples found sanctuary in the forest, as we often find it today in our gardens.

According to the wise ones in whose footsteps we are following, we don't have to *do* anything. We need only *be* wherever we find ourselves, in this case, in the sanctuary of our gardens. Right now, just bringing Mindfulness to the postures of the Body is enough. In so doing, we discover that meditation practice brings us to a new awareness of the Body.

SITTING MEDITATION

SOMETIMES WE GARDENERS SIT DOWN to weed, but only rarely do we find ourselves sitting for long. For many of us, practicing sitting meditation in the garden may be a new experience.

My sitting meditation is most likely to happen on the deck just before sunrise when the world around me is quiet. The air is often cool as I wrap a meditation shawl around my shoulders. I sit outdoors in March and April and again from July through October. In May and June, tiny biting blackflies as well as mosquitoes encourage me to sit indoors. My neighbor, Connie Woodberry, has solved this problem by having a screened-in porch where we meditate on weekend mornings.

Begin by choosing a comfortable place, one that is not too hot or cold or buggy. Find a bench that is not too hard or a cushion that is not too soft. And choose the time of day that is best for you and that is not likely to conflict with social demands.

Sitting quietly, doing nothing
Spring comes, and the grass grows by itself.

Zen poem

Introduction to Sitting Meditation

Sit as comfortably as you can. (If I cannot sit out-of-doors in a straight-backed porch chair, I like to meditate on a firm sofa, where I can sit cross-legged and yet have just a touch of back support.) If you are sitting cross-legged, the sit-bones should perch on the edge of the cushion in order to angle the knees down and provide support for them. A gardener's knees are important, so don't stress the knees by trying to place them in an uncomfortable position. If your knees stick up, switch to a chair with a straight back. Back support may be needed to protect that precious gardening tool, your Body. Some people prefer kneeling on a meditation bench.

Close your eyes gently or, without staring, allow the eyes to rest diffusely on a spot on the floor about five feet in front of you.

If you have already received sitting instructions from a meditation teacher, follow your usual format. Otherwise,

as the Body quiets down, bring the attention to the breath. Notice where the in-breath and the out-breath are most predominant—at the tip of the nose, at the chest, at the belly. Sometimes it helps to whisper in your Mind, "In. Out." or "Rising. Falling."

When your attention drifts, gently bring the focus back to the breath. Observe the in-breath. Observe the out-breath.

If the mind isn't yet still, just watch the in-and out-breath without trying to notice whether it's comfortable or not. Otherwise, the mind will start to stray. It's like a farmer planting an orchard: If he mows down too much grass all at once, he won't be able to plant all his trees in time and the grass will start growing again. He has to mow down just the area that he can plant in one day. That's how he'll get the results he wants.

Ajaan Lee Dhammadaro

Perhaps a meditation teacher has already recommended that you sit daily at a regular time in a space conducive to meditation. If you can, sit twice a day.

As an early bird, it took me decades to realize that my engines started running at 6:15 A.M. Sitting after that time was like trying to restrain wild horses. Since I needed to end my meditation by 6:15, I needed to get started at.... Well, you can do the math.

Sitting with a group (*sangha*) once a week can be a great support for your practice. If no meditation group exists near you, try to find just one other person to sit with every week. You will be amazed at the effect of such "companion planting."

Companion plants assist each other to grow well either because one supports the other or because each partner can repel the other's enemies.

I have been meditating every morning with my neighbors, ever since one, Connie, said to me in desperation, "I am so depressed. We have to start meditating again."

Connie and I had sat together weekly 18 years earlier, before her children were born. When her daughter was in high school, we began again—as we meditators always do in our practice. Sitting with one other person for 20 minutes a day not only steadied my practice, it deepened it, particularly as Connie and I began to report to each other how we were managing (or not!) to carry Mindfulness into our daily lives. A couple of years later, another neighbor joined us, and, two years after that, another.

This morning meditation group is the most precious gift I have ever received.

In the Shade Meditation

The Buddha said, "There is the case where a monk—having gone to the wilderness, to the shade of a tree—sits down folding his legs crosswise, holding his body erect and setting mindfulness to the fore. Always mindful he breathes in; mindful he breathes out. Breathing in a long breath, he knows, 'I am breathing in a long breath'; breathing out a long breath, he knows, 'I am breathing out a long breath'; breathing in a short breath, he knows, 'I am breathing in a short breath'; breathing out a short breath, he knows, 'I am breathing out a short breath.'"[4]

> *Do you have a favorite tree in your yard or in a nearby park? See if you can ensconce yourself comfortably on the ground beneath it. Or pull up a chair and sit in the shade under it. If you are sitting in a public place, you may wish to practice the eyes-half-open style of meditation.*
>
> *Place the attention on the breath, either at the tip of the nose or at the belly.*
> *Notice the in-breath. Notice the out-breath.*
> *Notice any long breaths. Notice any short breaths.*
> *Notice any deep breaths. Notice any shallow breaths.*
> *Notice any smooth breaths. Notice any bumpy breaths.*
> *Notice where the breath is comfortable. Notice where the breath is uncomfortable.*
> *What else do you notice about the breath?*

Green Loving–Kindness Meditation

As a gardener, you love plants, so try doing a Loving-Kindness Meditation to plants. (For an introduction to Goodwill and Loving-Kindness, see page 12).

Sitting comfortably in your yard or in a park and keeping your eyes partly open, allow your gaze to rest on a nearby plant, tree, or weed.

Say your Loving-Kindness phrases to this plant. "May you be safe. May you feel happy. May you feel strong. May you feel peaceful."

Spend a few minutes sending Loving-Kindness to your green "friend."

Beside Still Water Meditation

Sitting near a lake, a river, a stream, or the ocean can induce tranquility. Go out, now, to the water feature in your garden.

Sit next to a pond, a birdbath, or even a bowl of water with your eyes half-open, gazing at the water. Notice how still it is. Then feel where stillness resides within you.

You may feel that tranquility comes and goes. Maybe it only comes for one second. Notice it.

Keep your attention on the water for a few minutes.

Whenever mindfulness is there in sufficient force to clarify things, it makes the mind bright, it makes your wisdom clear. It's like putting water in a bowl. You can look into the bowl and see your face in it when the water is still and clean, just as with mindfulness you can see yourself.

Ajahn Chah

SENSATIONS
MEDITATIONS

Hearing Meditation

The garden abounds with sights, sounds, smells, tactile sensations, even tastes that stimulate your senses. You can use your five senses as focuses for meditation throughout the gardening day. Let's start with hearing:

> Bring your attention to any sounds around you: birdsongs or traffic, insects humming and buzzing, wind in the trees or the breeze created by your breath.
>
> Pay attention to the beginning of a sound and its end, although you will not necessarily hear the beginning of every sound or the end of every sound.
>
> Notice when a sound begins and follow it as it trails off into the last audible vibration.
>
> Focus on hearing, without trying to figure out what the sound is. Just label it softly in your Mind, "Hearing. Hearing."
>
> Notice the difference between your concept of the sound and the raw experience of the sound.
>
> Notice each sound as it arises and passes away.
>
> If there are no sounds, notice the sound of silence or return your attention to the breath.

Mind set free in the dharma-realm,
I sit at the moon-filled window
watching the mountains with my ears,
hearing the stream with open eyes.

Shutaku

29

Touch Meditation

Sitting comfortably, focus your attention on a tactile sensation. Notice your sit-bones resting on a cushion or chair. Feel the breeze on your skin. Or, if it's a very still day, can you feel the breath moving across your upper lip? Notice the weight of your hands on your legs or in your lap. Feel your feet or legs touching the ground. Pay attention to the sensation of your clothing touching your skin. Notice how the tongue sits in the mouth.

If an ache or pain announces itself, closely observe the sensation. Where exactly is it located? What are its qualities? Is it sharp or dull? Mild or strong? Warm or cool?

If no strong sensations arise, return the attention to the breath.

Texture Meditation

Gardening books tell us to vary the texture in the garden to increase visual interest, especially in monochromatic gardens. In the white garden at my front door I rely on texture and leaf form, as well as some annuals, to vary the mostly-green-leaved composition.

As you walk through your garden, touch the leaves of different plants. Notice the texture of each leaf—rough or smooth or hairy or sticky or bumpy or velvety or furry or spiny or prickly.

Place all your attention in your fingertips and notice the sensations of touching.

Continue practicing this meditation as you walk around your garden.

Gazing Meditation

If you've ever done a balance pose in yoga class, you know the importance of focusing on a spot on the wall. You also know that if the Mind drifts, the Body will too, and you will lose your balance. Just as gazing at a spot stills the Mind *and* Body, gazing with half-closed eyes relaxes the Body and quiets the Mind.

Sitting or standing comfortably, choose a flower as your outer still point. Soften the eyes and gaze into the flower, noticing its effect on your Mind and your Body.

Look deeply at the flower as if you are looking into the eyes of someone you love.

When the Mind wanders, gently return to gazing at the flower.

Meditation in the Scented Garden

On warm summer days, I love to lie in the path of my herb garden, nose at leaf level, breathing in the scent of lavender, oregano, and the mints growing profusely nearby.

If you have a scented garden, go out to it or to your herb garden. Sit among the fragrances, and if you feel comfortable, lie down, which will put you closer to the plants. Otherwise, pick a strongly scented flower or leaf and hold it close to your nose. Stand with your nose buried in the bark of a ponderosa pine. Sit and smell freshly mown grass.

You can also smell dirt, dry pine needles on a hot day, tomato leaves, or carrot fronds.

Settling in close to a garden fragrance—sitting, standing, or lying—notice the sensation of smelling. Where do you "feel" smelling?

Eating Meditation

Of course you can do eating meditation at least three times a day inside your home, but what better time to practice eating mindfully than when you're in the vegetable garden about to pop the season's first pea pod or cherry tomato into your mouth? Pull up a carrot, rub off the dirt, and crunch a bite (complete with trace minerals!).

Whatever you grow in your backyard, whether it be blueberries or oranges, lettuce or asparagus, try eating each fresh morsel you put into your mouth mindfully.

Bring awareness to all the sensations of gathering: the reaching, the twisting, the snipping, the tugging.

Notice your hand coming toward your mouth. Feel your salivary glands, the coursing of saliva. Be aware of your mouth opening and the fresh morsel touching lips, tongue, teeth. Smell any aroma. Feel your mouth closing. Notice the texture of the food. Notice your teeth biting. Notice the feel of the carrot, pea pod, cherry tomato on your tongue. Notice chewing and tasting.

Where exactly does the sensation of taste happen? At the back of your tongue? The front? Pay attention to the tongue. Notice swallowing. Where is your Mind?

Allow awareness to follow the tiniest details of eating as you enjoy your garden snack.

Edible Flower Meditation

I love to add nasturtiums, borage, and violas to a salad and surprise my dinner guests. Edible flowers offer visual *and* fragrant delights to any meal.

Pick a flower from the following list and very carefully eat it. Notice the texture, the smell. Notice chewing, tasting, swallowing. Notice the aftertaste.

nasturtiums
mint flowers
bee balm
broccoli
violas
pansy petals
violets
borage
chive blossoms
basil florets
marjoram flowers
oregano flowers
cilantro flowers
tulip petals
daylilies
lavender
squash blossoms (remove stamens)
chrysanthemum petals (blanched)
dandelion flowers (picked very young)
apple blossoms
red clover
yucca petals

pineapple guava
citrus blossom petals (use sparingly)
calendula
petunias
lilacs
carnation petals
rose petals
gladiola petals
scented geranium petals
chamomile
rosemary flowers
sage flowers
thyme flowers
lemon verbena
sweet woodruff flowers
savory flowers
hibiscus petals
dill flowers
primrose
linden flowers
okra flowers
honeysuckle flowers (berries are poisonous)
fennel flowers
hollyhock petals
burnet
sorrel
chicory petals
black birch twigs

All Senses Meditation

Now put all the senses together in one meditation, without choosing to focus on any one sense in particular.

> Sit comfortably in your garden, with your eyes closed or softly focused on the ground five feet in front of you. Be aware of sounds, smells, and tactile and other sensations.
>
> Direct your attention to whatever sense door opens. Hearing, touching, or smelling. The sounds in or around the garden. The sensations of sitting. Smell tomato leaves or the exhaust from traffic. Notice the difference between your concept of the experience and the raw experience itself.
>
> If nothing in particular draws your attention, return the attention to the breath.

I N BUDDHISM, THE MIND, TOO, is considered a sense door, although it is far more difficult to follow the Mind's movements than those emanating from the other five senses. Have you noticed how often and easily the Mind wanders? When, in the last Investigation, you were focused on hearing, feeling, touching, and perhaps even smelling, tasting, or seeing, where was the Mind? Was it on the sound of tires on gravel? A crow cawing? An ache in your back? Or did it turn to your "to do" list? Were you planning what to cook for dinner? Worrying about picking up your daughter after school and still making it to the library and post office before they close? Complaining to yourself about a co-worker?

In meditation practice we return again and again to the present moment. While the garden can be a pleasant setting for our practice, being present is not always easy. By now you've seen how easily the Mind strays. You've probably also experienced what some Buddhist teachers call "monkey mind." Instead of following a clear train of thought our Mind, like that of a monkey, seems to swing through the trees, leaping from one thought, worry, plan, complaint, or obsession to another. Often, despite our efforts to keep the Mind focused on observing the breath or a sensation, the Mind jumps capriciously and uncontrollably where *it* wants to go.

The saving grace is that the Mind can become aware of itself. You catch yourself. You bring the Mind back to the task at hand–watching the breath, noticing sensations, being aware that you are gardening.

When I ask gardeners, "Where does the Mind go while the Body is gardening?" most say that their Minds stay in the garden, with the sensations of gardening–

touching the earth, feeling the plants. The birder-gardener listens. The artist-gardener "frames" possible pictures to draw, paint, or photograph. The musical gardener hums or sings. Some gardeners say they feel quite Calm and peaceful in their gardens.

And the meditative gardener?

Where does your Mind go?

The Gardening Mind Meditation

Okay. Let's work with "monkey mind."

Take this book and a pencil out to the garden with you. Garden for one minute. Stop.

Jot down one-word notations of the things that crossed your Mind, for instance, planning, reviewing, designing, wondering, complaining, problem-solving, noticing. Perhaps the Mind doesn't stay in the garden, but wanders farther afield to remembering, imagining, worrying.

Garden for another minute and note down the ideas that went through your Mind.

Garden for five minutes.

Briefly write down what you can recall of your thoughts.

Pansy comes from the French word *pensée* meaning thought or remembrance.

There seems to be time only to look, note and look away. Outside pressures distract; nourishment for our mind and feelings becomes ever more meagre. It is a gardener's pleasure, as it could be the designer's privilege, to break this crazy rhythm, to change and break the rush of time, and make the garden a quiet island in which a moment has a new meaning.

Russell Page

This Shining Moment in the Now

When I work outdoors all day, every day, as I do now, in the fall,
getting ready for winter, tearing up the garden, digging potatoes,
gathering the squash, cutting firewood, making kindling, repairing
bridges over the brook, clearing trails in the woods, doing the last of
the fall mowing, pruning apple trees, taking down the screens,
putting up the storm windows, banking the house—all these things,
as preparation for the coming cold...

when I am every day all day all body and no mind, when I am
physically, wholly and completely, in this world with the birds,
the deer, the sky, the wind, the trees...

when day after day I think of nothing but what the next chore is,
when I go from clearing woods roads to sharpening a chain saw,
to changing the oil in a mower, to stacking wood, when I am
all body and no mind...

when I am only here and now and nowhere else—then, and only
then, do I see the crippling power of mind, the curse of thought,
and I pause and wonder why I so seldom find
this shining moment in the now.

David Budbill

WALKING MEDITATION[5]

A GARDENER WALKS CONSTANTLY—INSPECTING FLOWER beds, foraging for dinner greens, trudging back and forth to the compost pile. If you put on a pedometer, you'd be surprised how many steps you take while gardening. How many of those steps are even minimally mindful?

Perhaps you've learned walking meditation. Walking mindfully doesn't have to mean slowly. As you walk from your house to your garden, you won't be doing the slow motion-by-motion meditative walking that you may do on retreat or at a weekly meditation group.

You can do walking meditation any time you are in the garden. After all, gardening is simply walking—and bending over! Then walking some more, and bending over again.

For the first few hundred years after the death of the Buddha, he was represented not by a statue but by a footprint.

Basic Walking Meditation

Choose one element of walking—the feel of your heel striking the earth, the spring-board of your toes as the foot leaves the ground, the weightlessness of the foot moving through the air. If you are a barefoot gardener, notice the sensations of the soles of your walking feet. Hard, soft, tickly, rough, squishy, wet, damp, dry. Or notice the knee or the leg. Focus on one small part of the anatomy of walking and continue to pay attention to it as you make your usual circuit around your garden at your usual speed.

Here's another exercise you might try: Deliberately slow down your walking and pay attention to the motions themselves as you lift one foot, move it slightly, and place it on the ground. Then the other foot lifts, moves and places. While slow-ing down your movements, label them: "Lifting. Moving. Placing. Lifting. Moving. Placing."

Then resume your normal walking pace and label the sensations and move-ments of which you are aware as you walk. Find words that make sense to you. Do not worry over the label you choose. There are no right answers. Simply choose the first word that comes to Mind and whisper it very lightly in your Mind.

Practice some form of Walking Meditation when you are in the garden today.

Walking with Loving-Kindness

Is there a time of day when you stroll through your garden? Perhaps in the morning before work? Or after dinner, just before dusk? Choose a time when you walk for the sheer pleasure of enjoying your garden (and when weeding is least likely to distract you).

Recall the traditional Loving-Kindness meditation and the phrases which appeal to you. (See page 13.)

As you stroll through your garden, say your phrases in time to your walking. "May I feel safe," will probably last for four steps. "May I feel happy. May I feel strong. May I feel peaceful."

Repeat the phrases until you complete the circuit of your garden.

Gardener's Short-cut Meditation

Create a short-cut to your Loving-Kindness phrases. For example, "Safe. Happy. Strong. Peaceful."

With each footfall, say your one- or two-word short-cut. As you walk through your gardens pay attention to both your footfall and the well-wishing energy of your words. If you are walking quickly, each syllable may coincide with a footstep.

The path we're following is a short-cut. It's a path worn smooth. Following a smooth path means there are no weeds growing on it, no obstacles in our way, no need to stop here and there and slow down our progress.

Ajaan Lee Dhammadaro

STANDING
MEDITATION

WHEN WE THINK OF GARDENING, we think of an active Body in motion. Chances are, if we're standing still we're puzzling over something. "Hmm. How would that plant look from here?" or "I wonder if that area needs something." When our Minds are engaged in considering or planning, it is unlikely we'll notice that the Body is standing still.

I first learned standing meditation on retreat in Bodh Gaya, India, and it turned out to be very useful when standing in line for a train ticket for an hour and a half or waiting for the train for two hours.

. . .

Standing Meditation

Go out to your garden now and just stand still. Close your eyes, or, if that feels too unbalancing, crack your eyes open so you can see through your eyelashes. Allow the soft gaze to rest on a spot about a Body's length in front of you.

Spend a minute noticing the sensations of standing. Feel the upright stance of your Body, your torso lifted, your feet planted on the ground.

Spend another minute noticing the feet.

Spend a minute noticing the legs. Are the knees locked? Feel the strength of the thighs.

Notice that standing "still" is not entirely true. Perhaps an eye is fluttering or you're subtly shifting your weight from one foot to another. And, of course, you're breathing!

Take a minute to bring the attention to the breath.

Continue to practice this standing meditation for a few minutes.

Statue Meditation

Stand in front of a garden sculpture, perhaps a statue of the Buddha or St. Francis. Or if you have a tree with which you feel special kinship, stand near it and allow your gaze to rest on it.

Notice the sensations of standing.

•   •   •

Watering Your Practice

Watering your flowers with a hose and spray nozzle is a great opportunity to practice standing meditation.

As you are standing and watering your flowers, simply notice the sensations of standing. That way you can water your practice and your flowers at the same time.

LYING DOWN MEDITATION

Beautiful pictures in garden magazines and garden books notwithstanding, I seldom use the hammock, chaise longue, or even a bench for lying down. However, I can find my companion sunbathing on the terrace, surrounded by flowers, while I'm bent over a flower bed.

Body Scan[6]

Lie comfortably on your back, perhaps with a cushion under your knees, on the grass (if it's not too itchy and you're not concerned about ticks), a blanket, chaise longue, garden bench, or yoga mat. Bad backs may prefer the "astronaut position"—with the back on the ground and lower legs resting on the seat of a chair.

Take three breaths to settle yourself.

As you breathe in, notice the toes. As you breathe out, notice the balls of the feet.

As you breathe in, notice the arches of the feet. As you breathe out, notice the heels.

As you breathe in, notice the ankles. As you breathe out, notice the lower legs.

As you breathe in, notice the knees. As you breathe out, notice the thighs.

As you breathe in, notice the hips. As you breathe out, notice the buttocks.

As you breathe in, notice the groin. As you breathe out, notice the belly.

As you breathe in, notice the waist. As you breathe out, notice the lower back.

As you breathe in, notice the middle back. As you breathe out, notice the stomach.

As you breathe in, notice the upper back. As you breathe out, notice the chest.

As you breathe in, notice the shoulder blades. As you breathe out, notice the shoulders.

As you breathe in, notice the torso. As you breathe out, notice the legs and feet.

As you breathe in, notice the shoulders. As you breathe out, notice the upper arms.

As you breathe in, notice the elbows. As you breathe out, notice the lower arms.

As you breathe in, notice the wrists. As you breathe out, notice the backs of the hands.

As you breathe in, notice the palms of the hands. As you breathe out, notice the fingers.

As you breathe in, notice the shoulders. As you breathe out, notice the arms.

As you breathe in, notice the neck. As you breathe out, notice the ears.

As you breathe in, notice the chin. As you breathe out, notice the lips.

As you breathe in, notice the gums. As you breathe out, notice the tongue.

THE MEDITATIVE GARDENER

As you breathe in, notice the upper lip. As you breathe out, notice the nose.

As you breathe in, notice the cheeks. As you breathe out, notice the temples.

As you breathe in, notice the eyebrows. As you breathe out, notice the eyeballs.

As you breathe in, notice the forehead. As you breathe out, notice the scalp.

Breathe in from the top of your head and push the breath out through the bottoms of your feet.

Breathe in from the bottoms of your feet and push the breath out through the top of your head.

Allow the breath to return to normal.

Napping Meditation

I take a twenty-minute nap every afternoon or a power nap of six minutes—which may just be deep relaxation—if life is busy. When the weather warms up, taking a siesta in the garden can be delightful.

> *As you lie down in your yard or garden, gently close your eyes and rest your attention on the feel of the Body touching the ground or the bench.*
>
> *Notice any other sensations, such as a breeze cooling the skin or the heat of the sun.*
>
> *Notice any smells—of the grass, earth, flowers, or leaves.*
>
> *Notice any sounds around you. Really relax the sense of hearing, so that sounds are simply washing over you.*
>
> *Notice your response to any sound. Is there a tightening somewhere? Try to relax into simply hearing.*
>
> *Notice the breath.*
>
> *Do you fall asleep on an in-breath? Or an out-breath?*

Sitting, walking, standing, and lying down are the four basic positions of the Body. But just to cover any loopholes, the Buddha says,

"OR HOWEVER THE BODY IS DISPOSED..."

FAMILIAR GARDENERS' POSTURES INCLUDE BENDING over, squatting, and kneeling. Then there are positions determined by the use of tools—raking, shoveling, pruning, edging, clipping, mowing, and using a trowel. Mindfulness can be brought to all these postures in the garden.

The assignment sounds simple: Be mindful of the Body in the garden. But this moment-to-moment awareness is not easy when the Mind is accustomed to running loose.

Gardening Body Mindfulness Meditation

The next time you go out to your garden, keep bringing your attention back to the Body—walking, bending over, using tools. The Mind will wander away. Gently return it to the sensations of hearing, seeing, touching.

The Mind will drift again. Keep guiding your attention back to what you are doing. Mindfulness is another precious garden tool. Keep it sharpened.

When you are finished, congratulate yourself for doing this meditation, even if your total awareness added up to less than five seconds. You have exercised your Body and exercised Mindfulness.

Let the beauty we love be what we do.
There are a hundred ways to kneel and kiss the ground.

Rumi

Mindful Movement

Take your mindful movement practice out to the garden. Roll out a yoga mat in front of your favorite flower bed, and allow the natural energy of your garden to fill you. Practice Tai Chi or Qi Gong and see if you can sense the chi of the garden. Dancers can hold onto the tip of a tree branch and dance—mindfully—with a tree partner.

The Mindfulness Gardening "Room"

Several years ago, as an exercise, I decided to practice Mindfulness during my morning routine in the bathroom. Then I brought Mindfulness practice out-of-doors, to one of my garden "rooms," the shady walkway by the front door.

Choose a small section of your garden, not more than ten feet long, or a garden "room" if you have one.

Make a commitment to yourself to be as mindful as you can be every time you are in this part of the garden.

Practice for one season of gardening.

FEELINGS

IN English, the word "Feelings" (or "feeling") has many meanings. "Feelings" can mean, among others, emotions or tactile sensations or "a consciousness without regard to thought." For example, when you receive a "first impression," you instantly know how you feel even if you cannot articulate it. When you walk into a silent meditation retreat, you immediately know whom you like and whom you don't, even though you haven't talked to them.

In Pali, the word *Vedana* is usually translated as "feeling" and means feeling tone, not emotions. (In Buddhist psychology, emotions are considered "mental formations" and therefore part of Mind, the third foundation of Mindfulness.)

Vedanas are the "first impression" sort of Feelings—the simple responses of pleasant, unpleasant, and the neutral one of neither-pleasant-nor-unpleasant.

Human beings respond to their environment in three ways: Attraction or desire toward the pleasant; resistance or pushing away from the unpleasant; and a neutral "so-so." Even a slug recognizes pleasant and unpleasant. It is attracted by sugar water (which some people use as a trap) and repelled by wood ash or sawdust.

These Feelings are short-lived, lasting a few seconds or less. When you look at your favorite flower, how long can you maintain the feeling of "pleasant" before pleasantness fades or your attention turns elsewhere?

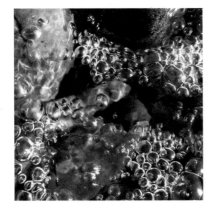

In us, there is a river of feelings in which every drop of water is a different feeling.

Thich Nhat Hanh

Vedanas Quiz

(There are no wrong answers.)

Quickly put a check mark in the column which most closely describes your Feelings. If you can't decide, leave it blank and move on to the next item

	Pleasant	Unpleasant	Neutral or Ambiguous
cool			
warm			
hot			
shade			
full sun			
misty rain			
rain			
thunderstorms			
lightning			
wind			
breeze			
sweating			

	Pleasant	Unpleasant	Neutral or Ambiguous
dirt under your fingernails			
gloves			
dry hands			
flowers			
vegetables			
weeds			
fences			
digging a hole for a shrub			
buying plants			
planting plants			
planting bulbs			
planting seeds			
transplanting			
harvesting			
dead-heading			
weeding			
watering			
setting up the sprinkler			
rolling up the hose			
irrigation system			

	Pleasant	Unpleasant	Neutral or Ambiguous
pruning			
clipping a hedge			
mowing			
edging			
compost pile			
turning over the compost pile			
laying down mulch			
applying deer repellants			
fertilizing			
snakes			
worms			
bugs			
bees			
butterflies			
hummingbirds			
mosquitoes			
pond fish			
snails			

	Pleasant	Unpleasant	Neutral or Ambiguous
slugs			
birds			
birdsongs			
chipmunks			
squirrels			
deer			
pests			
applying pesticide			
picking bugs off plants			
having organized tools			
organizing your tools			
pushing a wheelbarrow			
pulling a garden cart			

Now that you are aware of Feelings, you can use them as an object of your meditation today, tomorrow, and the next day.

Flower Bed Meditation

The teacher of a landscape gardening class asked us to stand in our flower beds at home and notice how we felt. Standing in one steep hillside garden, I realized I didn't like being there. No wonder I seldom got around to weeding that bed.

Go out and stand in one of your flower beds. Yes. Just stand there, inside the flower bed.

Look around. How do you feel here? Pleasant? Unpleasant? Or neutral?

Stand in another flower bed. How does it feel?

Feelings Meditation

Sit comfortably in your garden noticing whatever comes into your field of awareness. Label each sound, sensation, breath, or thought as "Pleasant," "Unpleasant," or "Neutral."

What wonderful things a garden can do all by itself and
what endless pleasure it gives as it makes all its changes!

Elisabeth Sheldon

• • •

Feeling the Garden Meditation

As you walk around your garden, look at each plant and whisper how you feel about it: "Pleasant," "Unpleasant," or "Neutral."

Look at each of your tools and say how you feel about it: "Pleasant," "Unpleasant," or "Neutral."

• • •

Weeding Meditation #1

As you weed your garden today, use the words, "Pleasant," "Unpleasant," or "Neutral" to label each weed you see and each weed you pull.

L ET'S FACE IT. IT'S EASIER to meditate if you are in pleasant surroundings. The heart is relaxed and happy, and perhaps a half-smile comes to the lips. So the garden can be an excellent place to meditate.

However if unpleasant Feelings keep popping up ("Ooh, there's a weed" or "Is that a Japanese beetle?" or "Hmm. I really should move that plant."), it may be wiser to narrow your focus onto something pleasant. Or go sit in someone else's garden or in a park where you have nothing to do.

By making yourself comfortable when you begin sitting, you are less likely to be distracted by pain or irritated by discomfort. As we age, the Body may not go into all the positions it once did; sitting in a chair or on a bench may be more comfortable for inflexible joints than sitting on a cushion.

Nevertheless, pain will eventually come up. Sooner or later, everyone has an opportunity to notice such Feelings (unpleasant, unpleasant) and the attendant sensations (dull, sharp, mild, strong, hot, cool). In fact, pain can help create deeper Concentration, while too much comfort may induce sluggishness.

Meditation on a Slug

The next time you find a slug or other creepy-crawler in your garden, notice the feeling of repulsion. If you can, locate in the Body that feeling of "Get it out of here" or "I don't want to look."

Notice if the Mind has already begun plotting ways to deal with the slug problem.

Stop.

Look at the slug again. Maybe even touch it.

Can you find the Feeling of "unpleasant" that comes before the desire to get rid of the slug or move away from it? Can you find the Feeling that comes before the Mind gets busy?

THE FEELING-CRAVING TWO-STEP

RECENTLY, A PALE PINK *PULMONARIA* (lungwort) seized my attention as I entered the salon where I get my hair cut. I thought to myself "beautiful" (pleasant) and then, "I've got to have it." (Craving.) I have other Pulmonaria in my shade garden and was desperate to acquire this one. I wanted the plant so badly, I could think of nothing else. I peppered the salon owner with questions, hoping she would offer me a cutting. When she didn't, I went right home, and found Pierre's Pure Pink Pulmonaria on the internet. I then added it to a list of "plants I want" on my palm pilot. That's how strong the Craving was.

Sometimes a Craving can be so strong, as mine was for the Pulmonaria, that one scarcely notices the Feeling that generated it. In this case, a Feeling of pleasant. Unpleasant Feelings also generate Craving—that whatever it is that's disagreeable to us will end, and the sooner the better! This little two-step process of Feeling and Craving[7] is jammed so closely together in our daily experience, it's hard to notice the details of the transition. Yet, being aware of Feelings—pleasant, unpleasant, or neutral—will help us to observe what happens next in the Mind.

Investigation on Watching the Feeling–Craving Two-Step

The best place to notice Craving is when it arises right after a Feeling.

> *The next time you are in the garden, begin by noticing Feelings—pleasant, unpleasant, and neutral. What happens immediately after a Feeling of pleasant? What happens after a Feeling of unpleasant? Do you crave that the Feeling of pleasant will go on and on? That a Feeling of unpleasant will end immediately?*
>
> *If it's winter, look through your pile of garden catalogs, especially those with lots of colorful pictures. As you thumb through them, look at each picture and name the Feeling that goes with it. "Pleasant," "Unpleasant," or "Neutral." Notice when desire strikes.*
>
> *Continue to notice the moment-to-moment changes of Feeling (and perhaps Craving) as you turn the pages.*

MIND

OUR MINDS ARE A JUNGLE of exotic greenery that we walk or run through every day without really recognizing what it is that grows there. We may even develop a certain fondness for some plants that we later find out have poisonous roots.

Learning to distinguish beneficial thoughts from stressful thoughts allows us to identify the native flora of our Minds. The precursor to this identification is Mindfulness. We have to look closely, sometimes with the hand lens of moment-to-moment awareness, to really identify what we are observing in our Minds.

In the spring everything needs to be done at once—now—and can't wait. We dash about, frequently intending to perform a certain task, then finding ourselves dealing with five or six others on our way to the first. For example, the list of "Spring Jobs" says: "1. Divide Chelone. Put division in empty space by 'Seafoam'." Good. You get your tools and pry out the Chelone, trot with it down to the designated spot in the border where you discover that a double saponaria has sneakily moved in to annex all the ground around 'Seafoam'. You go for a large plastic bag and fill it with saponaria you've forked up. Where to plant it. You notice an empty space by a shed, near a clematis—but oh! The clematis has fallen and needs attention. Back to the house for hammer, hooks, and twist ties. On the way, you notice that the weeding and edging must be done immediately if there is to be a garden this year at all. The day had started off cold; now it's hot. You must go in to take off your wool tights and put on blackfly repellent, a hat, sunscreen (on top of or under the insect repellent?), and dark glasses. The sun is searing now, but rain is predicted, or possibly snow. But good heavens! Where did you leave that Chelone?

Elisabeth Sheldon

Lately, if you've been paying more attention to where the Mind goes, what have you noticed?

Chances are the Mind has been thinking about the past or the future. Even if it stays in the garden, it is often planning what to do next, wondering about what's been done so far, measuring progress, admiring some plants, sighing about others.

My Mind often ranges further afield to the book I'm reading or the movie I saw last night. Sometimes my Mind indulges in a bit of gossip about people or it reviews recent conversations. Sometimes it waters the seeds of Suffering by chewing on problems at work or family issues or maybe it's day-dreaming. Once in a while, the Mind waters wholesome thoughts and actions by being Calm, awake, and mindful of being in the garden and in the Body as it is gardening.

Mind and Body Contemplation

Consider the relationship between Mind and Body in the garden.

How does your Mind relate to the garden? What about the Body? What does your Mind say about your garden? What does your Body "say"?

Where is the Body? Where is the Mind?

How are Mind and Body different? How are they similar?

How does Mind relate to Body? How does Body relate to Mind?

Ask these questions to yourself near the end of your daily meditation or while you are gardening. Just let the questions drop into the pool of your awareness and notice if any insights ripple out. An answer may not come immediately or even anytime soon. Continue to ask these questions and continue to listen.

Return to this contemplation on Mind and Body throughout the gardening season.

THE THREE ROOTS OF STRESS: GREED, AVERSION, AND DELUSION

GARDENERS KNOW WHAT TO DO with roots. You plant nice ones and feed and water them so they grow and support a vigorous plant.

If you want to get rid of a weed, you pull it up by its roots. Merely pulling off the leaves gives only temporary aesthetic results. Occasionally you have to get the shovel and dig out a taproot. If you have clay-ey soil, you may need a weeder to pry out even a single blade of unwanted grass. Sometimes you have to cover a bed with black plastic to kill off an invasive weed and its roots.

In our meditation practice, we meditator-gardeners face the challenge of uprooting unwholesome thoughts and actions that cause Stress or Suffering. The Buddha identified Three Roots of Stress: Greed, Aversion, and Delusion.

When we experience Greed or desire (or its relatives clinging or attachment), we want a pleasant state to continue or want something we don't have. "I wish the irises would bloom longer." "I want perfect weather." "I wish it would rain only at night." "I want more time to spend in my garden."

Seized by Aversion or hatred, we want one thing: an end to what is unpleasant. Sometimes Aversion can be recognized by its strong opinions. "I hate this rain and want it to stop!" "Weeds! They're ruining my garden." "I have never liked magenta flowers."

Delusion or ignorance, on the other hand, causes us to wonder, "Is this a weed or not?" "Should I move this plant or leave it here?" "Am I doing this right?" Delusion is very pervasive; it underlies both Greed and Aversion.

The Roots of Stress are so strong that in the Tibetan tradition they are sometimes called the Three Poisons because they pollute our lives.

All of us suffer Mind states and behaviors arising from Greed, Aversion, and Delusion, but often one Mind state or root predominates. In Buddhist circles, perhaps you've heard people say: "She tends to be aversive." "He's a greedy type." "I'm a deluded type." Buddhist psychology describes three personality types based on the inclinations of our Minds—toward Greed, Aversion, or Delusion.

I have found this typology to be helpful in my relationships with other people. I use the words lightly and quietly to myself, in a way that deepens my understanding of others' idiosyncrasies as well as my own. To say these words disparagingly would be cultivating Aversion, and I already have quite enough of those aversive weed-thoughts in my Mind.

Are there flowers you can think of that fit into these categories? Mint, bee balm, and other such spreading plants could be termed "Greedy" because in their exuberance they tend to take over a garden. Roses and globe thistle are beautiful, but their prickliness might cause them to be called "Aversive." That label doesn't mean we like them any less. Perhaps *Nicotiana* (flowering tobacco) could be termed "Delusional" for its intoxicating evening scent, the nicotine properties of its leaves, and its ability to self-seed and multiply. If we have toyed with any addiction we know very well that "delusional" state of "This little bit won't hurt me."

"We" are like a tree. "Attachment" is like vines. If we feel desire for sights, they'll wind around our eyes. If we feel desire for sounds, they'll wind around our ears and so forth. When we're all tangled up like this, we'll have to die.

Ajaan Lee Dhammadaro

Roots of Stress Quiz

Does your Mind incline toward Greed? Aversion? Delusion? Even in the garden, where so many of us find refuge, we can identify Mind states and behaviors arising from the Three Roots of Stress or Suffering. If we pay attention, we may discover that our gardening habits indicate a certain tendency of our personalities.

Circle the letter next to the answer that most closely applies to you.

G I always store my trowel in the same place.

A I leave my trowel lying around.

D Hmmm. I don't remember where I left my trowel.

G My tools are organized.

A My tools are in a jumble.

D Tools?

G My tools are color-coordinated.

G My garden gloves are color-coordinated with my garden boots (or garden clogs).

A I never wear gloves.

D I can't find my gloves.

G My flowers beds are color-coordinated.

D I don't understand how anyone color-coordinates a flower bed.

G I'm hesitant to divide my perennials.

A I don't like my plants to touch each other.

G I can't bear to throw plants out.

A If a plant doesn't perform, I get rid of it.

D I can't decide what to do with extra plants.

G My beds are neatly edged.

A I don't like to edge my flower beds.

D My edges blend in with the lawn.

G My plants are neatly ordered from short in front to tall in back.

A I never plant in rows.

G My garden is pretty much under control.

A My garden looks like a jungle by July.

D I'm not sure what's a plant and what's a weed.

G I work on one bed. When it's in good shape, I move on to the next.

A I work on several flower/vegetable beds at the same time.

G I sow seeds exactly as the packet directs.

A I scatter seeds without even reading the packet.

G I use string to mark the rows of seeds.

A I mark a row of seeds with a stick.

D I sort of forget where I sowed my rows of seeds.

G I would call myself a careful gardener.

D I don't know what kind of gardener I am.

G I often sweep my sidewalk (or garden path).

A I never sweep my sidewalk.

D Should I sweep my sidewalk?

G I love to water my flower beds or vegetable garden.

A Rolling out the hose is such a drag.

D I'm not sure when to water.

G I like to garden when the weather is perfect.

A I garden in all sorts of weather.

D I just happen to find myself out in the garden.

D I don't plan what I'm going to do in the garden until I get out there.

G I sometimes wear protective eye-wear when I'm gardening.

A Protective eye-wear? That is going too far.

D I never heard of anyone protecting their eyes while gardening.

A I just want to get it done.

G I receive scads of flower or vegetable catalogs.

G I collect varieties of a specific species.

G I like to have one of everything.

D I try to grow things outside their recommended climate zone.

A I know the names of almost all the plants I grow.

D I don't know the names of a lot of plants.

A I love gardens but I don't really like gardening.

G I plant according to the date on the seed packet.

A I plant earlier than the date on the seed packet.

D I don't seem to get around to planting until June.

G I get rid of bugs as soon as they appear.

A I ignore the bugs in my garden.

D I seldom notice bugs in my garden.

THE MEDITATIVE GARDENER

Now count up your score:

    G_____   A_____   D_____

This quiz is by no means scientific, but it may provide a clue about your habits of Mind. Greed wants a pleasant state to continue. Aversion wants an unpleasant state to stop. Delusion may be lost and confused in a state of neither pleasant nor unpleasant.

The trick is not to berate yourself for exhibiting a tendency toward Greed, Aversion, or Delusion. Being averse to Aversion, for instance, just waters the seeds of Aversion and creates more of it, not less—sort of like scratching poison ivy.

We all have all of the roots, so have as much Compassion for yourself as you would have for your best friend. Remember: your best friend still loves you despite your main Root of Suffering.

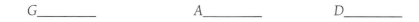

> There is no lotus flower possible without the mud.
> There is no understanding and compassion
> without suffering.
>
> Thich Nhat Hanh

Lotus Visualization

A lotus grows with its roots in the mud, its stem and bud growing up through the sometimes murky or scummy water. When the lotus blooms, its flower head rises above the water. We too can rise above our flaws and the Stresses of life.

Imagine that you are a lotus seed buried in the mud beneath a lotus pond. Feel the mud around you.

With a determined heart, you begin to wriggle in the earth. You extend your roots deep, deep into the mud. Then, a little shoot breaks through the mud. Your new green shoot grows up slowly through the murky water. Your stem grows higher and higher, taller and taller. A bud begins to form at the tip of this shoot which slowly reaches upward.

At last your bud reaches the surface of the water. Warmed by the sun, it swells and slowly opens.

Finally the flower is fully open—a perfect lotus. Look closely at this beautiful flower. What color is it? White, red or pink, blue-purple, or pale yellow?

Feel the full extent of your lotus Body rooted in the mud, subject to various currents, finally flowering in the sun and fresh air.

Lotus leaves have a self-cleaning mechanism called the Lotus Effect. Lotus leaves don't get wet. Instead, water rolls off the leaf like mercury, taking mud, microscopic particles, and tiny insects with it. Although lotuses prefer to grow in muddy rivers and lakes, the leaves and flowers remain clean.

Y OU CAN LEARN TO RECOGNIZE the off-shoots of the Roots of Stress. Only then can you consider the possibility of reducing the water you give to the roots and the seeds of Greed, Aversion, and Delusion. Withholding nourishment is not easy as these lifelong habits of Mind have voracious roots, like the graceful weeping willow that invades water pipes hidden underground.

Botanists classify plants into Families. For instance the Rose (*Rosaceae*) family, whose characteristic is five-petaled flowers (think wild roses), includes strawberries (*Fragaria*), the entire *Prunus* genus (plums, apricots, peaches, cherries, and almonds), roses, the bramble berries such as raspberries and blackberries (*Rubus*), apples and pears, spireas and potentillas.

The very useful Potato family (*Solanaceae*) includes peppers (*Capsicum*), tobacco (*Nicotiana*), *Datura*, all the *Solanums* (potatoes, nightshades, tomatoes, eggplant) and *Petunia*.

The strongly-flavored Mustard or Cabbage family (*Brassicaceae*) includes mustard, cresses (edible and flowering), and radishes, as well as all the *Brassicas* (broccoli, cauliflower, cabbage, Brussels sprouts, kale, collards, Chinese cabbage), *Nasturtium,* and *Wasabi*.

The Aster family (*Asteraceae*) is made up of composite flowers and includes yarrow (*Achillea*), artemisia, and thistle, as well as asters, lettuce, dandelions, and goldenrods.

We can think of Greed, Aversion, and Delusion as Families also.

We have arrived here, on this earth, with six roots, three wholesome and three unwholesome. The roots of unwholesomeness are greed, hatred, and delusion; the roots of wholesomeness are generosity, love, and wisdom....

Recognizing which of the six roots we are dealing with at the moment is crucial because we have to cut down the weeds or cherish and care for the flowers. One of the six roots is always at work.

Ayya Khema

Identifying the Species

Can you add a member or two to any of these Families?

Greed	Aversion	Delusion
desire	anger	dreaming
yearning	irritation	fantasizing
wanting more	dislike	wishy-washy
covetousness	impatience	spacing out
bragging, boasting	disappointment	Pollyanna
selfishness	disgust	"I want to chew it over."
conceit	judgments	absent-minded
laughing every few minutes	sarcasm, wry, ironic	scatter-brained
		fuzzy
pride	shame	guilt
"It's all good."	"Whatever."	"No problem."
binging	purging	anorexia
bewitched	bothered	bewildered
_____	procrastination	_____
_____	shyness	_____
_____	complaining	_____
_____	_____	_____
_____	_____	_____

While you will not be able to fill out the rest of this chart today, return to it from time to time, as Greedy, Aversive, or Delusional characteristics occur to you, and add them to the list.

Have Patience.

Remember: you are learning to identify mental weeds one at a time. Like the weeds in our gardens, mental weeds are not always easy to recognize. Identification takes time and commitment. I spent years in my flower and vegetable gardens before taking the time to identify some of the most common weeds there. I only just learned what ragweed looks like and I've been allergic to it for more than 50 years!

Lotus Loving-Kindness

Imagine yourself sitting in the middle of a beautiful lotus flower. Rest there for a moment.

Now say to yourself, "I love myself as I am." Say the words even if you doubt their truth.

Say, "I love myself as I am, _____(fill in the blank)_____." Fill in the blank with qualities from the list above in Identifying Species or other traits you deem to be unlovable or even downright wrong. For instance, "I love myself as I am, confused." "I love myself as I am, annoyed." "I love myself as I am, lustful." "I love myself as I am, opinionated." "I love myself as I am, bad." "I love myself as I am, feeling guilty." "I love myself as I am, hopeless." "I love myself as I am, feeling unlovable."

Continue to fill in the blank with present emotions or characteristics until you can't think of any more.

Then say, "I love myself as I am. I love and accept myself just as I am."

Now that you can recognize a few of your mental and behavioral weeds, you'll be able to observe their growth habits more closely.

Here in New England, I have a four-year-old flower bed where dozens of violets keep popping up. They meet the definition for a weed as they are growing where I don't want them to grow. However, since they are colorful and sweet, I refrain from pulling them out until after they've finished blooming (and gone to seed) in May. By July I have a new crop of violets.

Your Mind is a garden,
your thoughts are the seeds.
The harvest can be
either flowers or weeds.

When you can notice your mental, verbal and other habits in action, you'll be able to decide whether you really want to continue cultivating the nettles of off-the-cuff opinions, the violets of shyness, the bindweeds of envy and desire or the jimsonweeds (*Datura*) of Delusion. Over time, you may be able to thin out some of the smaller unwholesome habits of Mind, much as you pull up unwanted weeds from your garden. Eventually someone may say to you, as a friend said to me, "You used to be an angry person. What happened?"

In the first year of my garden, I planted four Alberta spruces, one at each corner. Forty years later, in the summer of 2002, after much anguish, I decided to take out the one occupying the southeast corner. It had grown to twenty feet and dominated the entrance, almost entirely blocking the path....

It took maybe fifteen minutes for them to cut it down. It came down all in one piece. The root system took longer to hack out than that one decisive cut through the trunk—one can easily sense the metaphorical resonance in that.

Stanley Kunitz

Once in a while, though, you find a deep-rooted weed and have to bring out all the tools of your meditation practice (and perhaps the help of a psychotherapist) to begin to dig around the roots.

Beginning gardeners often aim for the clean-dirt look surrounding plants. After all, that's the way British gardens and botanical gardens look, they tell themselves. (Do we hear a hint of Delusion here? The idea that weeds won't grow in "clean" soil is a pure wish. If weeds aren't visible in British and botanical gardens, it's because such places have enough gardeners on staff to pull them.) Years of experience finally convince many of us that we can never keep up with the weeding. That's why veteran gardeners sing the one-note song: "Mulch!" Mulch not only keeps weeds down, it acts as humus, improving the soil for the plants we do want to grow.

Mindfulness has a similar effect on our Minds. It helps us become aware of our mental weeds and thereby make our Minds more fertile ground in which to grow beautiful qualities of the Mind, such as happiness, Joy, or tranquility.

And just as mulch retains moisture and keeps the soil cooler in hot weather and warmer in cold weather, Mindfulness can keep us cooler in hot-tempered situations and just a little warmer in cold, depressing times.

When mental weeds do sprout, you still have to identify them. But then, after recognizing a weed of unskillful thought or action, you will have built up a bit of mental muscle. So, when weeds still appear, they can be easily pulled up (especially if the mulching has happened for a few years).

Simply recognizing a mental weed exposes its roots and shoots to the strong sunlight of Mindfulness. Sometimes no further action is required, as you watch an unskillful thought or action simply wither.

As gardeners have paraphernalia such as black plastic or landscaping fabric to suppress unwanted weeds, we meditators have effective means to keep down mental weeds. But we need to make sure that we are suppressing, rather than repressing, the Roots of Suffering.

Psychologically speaking, repression means the roots are still there, just waiting to spring forth when given an opening–a moment of unconscious mindlessness, for example, when a slip of the tongue reveals feelings that are too embarrassing to own.

Suppression, or biting your tongue, on the other hand, deliberately inhibits the growth of unwanted weeds or unkind words. Even though a weed springs up in the Mind, it is not expressed through words or actions. However, suppressing words or actions and "stuffing" feelings is like stuffing a baked potato: you can never fit everything back inside and just close it up. Suppressing unskillful words and actions while at the same time being mindful of the unwanted or difficult feelings or thoughts that have arisen is called radical acceptance.[8] This is where the mental muscle you've been building by exercising Mindfulness comes in handy as you note, "Irritation. Irritation." "Tightness." or "Craving. Craving." "Leaning toward." "Leaning into."

> When we practice, our effort is to water positive seeds and let the negative seeds remain dormant. We don't say, "Until I've gotten rid of all my bad seeds, I can't practice." If you get rid of all your unwholesome seeds, you won't have anything to practice. We need to practice now with all the unwholesome seeds in us. If we don't, the negative seeds will grow and cause a great deal of suffering.
>
> Thich Nhat Hanh

Another method of weed control consists of depriving weeds of nourishment. The soil in our flower gardens can contain as many as 80,000 weed seeds per square yard. By applying water directly to our perennials and vegetable plants, rather than soaking our entire gardens, we fail to water weed seeds and the weeds will fail to grow.

So, too, with the Mind. Try watering wholesome seeds and not watering unwholesome seeds. For instance, if you know that going to the garden center is going to feed desire, don't go. Or, put on blinders, pick up what's on your list, and walk directly to the check-out counter. If you know that something causes Aversion, don't pay attention to it, don't nourish it. Don't look at the magenta and orange flower bed if you can't stand that color combination.

When you notice, in hindsight, that your usual weed—Greed, Aversion, or Delusion—has sprung up, don't berate yourself. (Remember: Getting down on yourself waters the seeds of Aversion.) Applying Round-up or an herbicide has the effect of killing off weeds but can also inadvertently kill neighboring plants that you

do like or other plants of which you may not even be aware. Instead, review what happened; forgive yourself as you would a young puppy, and resolve to act differently next time. Remember: we are training our Minds. This is a practice and we need to practice. We need to weed our mental gardens. Have you ever met anyone who didn't have to weed?

So. What are you going to plant in place of unwholesome habits?

The Three Roots of Stress are counterbalanced by Three Wholesome Roots. Specifically, the antidote to Greed is Generosity. The antidotes to Aversion are Loving-Kindness and Compassion. The antidote to Delusion is Wisdom itself.

•   •   •

Watering the Roots of Wisdom

Go back to the Roots of Stress quiz, on page 77. What was your highest score?

If it was Greed, commit to practicing Generosity for a day.

If it was Aversion, commit to practicing Loving-Kindness and Compassion for a day.

If it was Delusion, commit to sitting meditation and reading two pages of a meditation book during one day. (This book counts!)

THE PERFECTIONS

WHEN WE PRACTICE THE PERFECTIONS (or Paramis) we cultivate the whole-some roots of thought and action. As a filter purifies the water we drink, the practice of the Perfections purifies our thought and action. The qualities we are practicing and seeking to perfect are:

Generosity
Virtue
Renunciation
Wisdom
Energy
Patience
Truthfulness
Determination
Loving-Kindness
Equanimity

They are called paramis, from parama which means supreme. We have their seed in us. If that were not so, we would be cultivating barren ground.

Ayya Khema

Generosity (*Dana*)

Generosity (*dana*) stands first in the list of Perfections (*Paramis*) to be developed. This is because cultivating Generosity opens the heart while also giving us practice in non-attachment.

Every time you give away a plant, a cutting, or some seeds, you are practicing Generosity.

In 1916, Guido von Webern bought some property in Dayton, Ohio, and found a clump of unusual double bloodroot (*Sanguinaria canadensis multiplex*). He gave four pieces of it away. Several years later, the original clump disappeared, and only the Arnold Arboretum in Boston had a specimen. The other three recipients had also lost their plants. Thanks to Guido von Webern's Generosity, we gardeners can now buy and enjoy this lotus-looking little wildflower.

Generosity has the added advantage of being the antidote to Greed. If you scored high on Greed on the Roots of Stress quiz (page 77), you might try taking on the practice of Generosity for a day or a week or a month. Besides plants, seeds, and cuttings, you can give away compliments. Thank people who perform simple services for you. Give a glass of water to the person who mows your lawn (even if he is related to you). Offer to weed a flower bed for an elderly neighbor. Volunteer to work with a community garden. Take a bouquet to someone in a nursing home. Take some of your surplus vegetables to a food shelf or a soup kitchen. If you live on a street frequented by walkers or runners or traffic, make your front yard garden into a gift to passers-by.

Flower Garden in Your Heart Visualization[10]

Put your attention on the breath for just a few moments.

Imagine a luxuriant flower garden with exquisite blooms and fragrances growing in your heart, cultivated by your love and Compassion. Enjoy the garden in your heart and all the flowers in it, feeling a sense of ease and well-being.

Now cut a bouquet of the loveliest flowers you can find, and hand it to your most beloved person. Express your love through this gift.

Think of your parents, whether they're alive or not. Make the most beautiful bouquet out of the flowers in your heart and hand it to them with your love, gratitude, and devotion. See the Joy that it brings them.

Consider those people who are nearest and dearest to you, with whom you might live, and for each of them make a spectacular bouquet nourished by your love; give each of them the gift that comes from your heart without expecting anything in return.

Now think of all your good friends, relatives, acquaintances, anyone who comes to Mind. Give each of them a special bouquet from the garden in your heart, nourished by your love and compassion.

Picture the people you meet in your daily life—neighbors, students, teachers, patients, salespeople, letter carriers, anyone who comes to Mind. Realize that the

more flowers you give away the more will soon grow in your heart. You can make a beautiful bouquet for each of these people with the loveliest blooms you can find, and you can give them the gift that comes straight from your heart.

Now think of a difficult person in your life, a person whom you reject and resist, or who rejects you. If you can't think of anyone, picture someone toward whom you feel indifferent, whom you neither like nor dislike. Cut an exquisite bouquet and hand it to that person with love and respect and care. See the Joy that it produces and the relief you feel.

Open your heart as wide as you can and extend the flower garden to its largest possible degree. Then allow people to enter and enjoy the flowers. Encourage each person to take home a flower from your bountiful garden.

Allow all those in your neighborhood to come into the garden of your heart, which is nourished by love, looked after by care and concern. As each visitor takes one of the beautiful blooms, a new one grows in its place. See the Joy that this brings. Then allow others in the community to come and enjoy the experience. Feel loved as you give the gift of a flower from your heart. Think of your hometown and the people you know and have seen there and those whom you imagine live there; let them all enter the garden of your heart, and give each one a bloom. Observe the happiness this brings them.

Picture all the people whom you have met anywhere at any time, seen anywhere at any time, or heard about, and let them each enter and take away with them a beautiful flower from the garden of your heart.

As you open your heart ever more, and as the garden becomes larger and larger, let all the living beings whom you can think of enter, be joyful, and be given the gift of a flower. Share with them a feeling of our togetherness.

Turn the attention back on yourself as you see that the flower garden in your heart is unimpaired. There are just as many blooms now as there were to start with. Giving away flowers has certainly not diminished them; their fragrance and beauty bring Joy to your heart and cause you to feel a sense of well-being, to feel surrounded by love.

Now anchor that flower garden in your heart so that you have access to it at any time and never lose it.

May people everywhere become aware of the radiant flowers in their own hearts.

THE MEDITATIVE GARDENER

G ENEROSITY HAS TWO SIDES: GIVING and receiving. Learning to receive with an open heart is as important as learning to give in an open-handed manner. A friend gave me a pink lily-of-the-valley shortly after I had decided that lily-of-the-valley spread much too vigorously. I had just ripped it all out of my garden, except for one self-contained bed. My friend was very excited about this gift. I tried to be appreciative, but I felt the stretch of trying to be grateful for something I didn't want. By focusing on my own wants and desires and not recognizing her open-heartedness, I missed an opportunity to transplant her Joy into my own heart.

Receiving a gift graciously allows the giver to experience the Joy of giving. Joy is such a wholesome emotion, it is so beneficial, that it is one of the Seven Factors for Awakening. Joy can wake us up.

Generosity is the soil out of which loving-kindness and compassion grow and flower.

Bhikkhu Khantipalo

Exercising Generosity

"You multiply your plants by dividing them." I love gardener's math because it is counter-intuitive.

List three things from your garden that you can easily give away.

If nothing comes to Mind, continue to consider this question as you walk around your garden today.

Think about something that you had trouble receiving.
   Can you remember something that you received open-heartedly? How did the giver respond?

Virtue

Soon after I moved into my new house in Vermont, my mother sent me "wildflowers in a can." Oh, boy! My garden could look like the label! Yet just shaking the seeds over an area gave disappointing results. Had I read the instructions carefully, I would have realized that the ground needed to be prepared in order for the flowers to grow and flourish.

Likewise, the seeds of Generosity, Loving-Kindness, and Wisdom will have a difficult time sprouting in our inner landscapes if our lives are not grounded in ethical precepts. In the Buddhist tradition, practitioners are encouraged to follow Five such Precepts, which express the integrity of Virtue. They are:

> I will be mindful and not destroy or harm living creatures.
> I will be mindful and not take that which is not offered.
> I will be mindful and refrain from sexual misconduct.
> I will be mindful and refrain from incorrect speech.
> I will be mindful and refrain from mind-clouding intoxicants which can lead to carelessness.

Following the Precepts helps us carry into our daily lives the Calm and peace we find in our gardens. Taking this ethical stance also supports our efforts to cause less Suffering to ourselves and others. (For a more complete discussion of the Precepts, see pages 119 to 142.)

Five Precepts Investigation

Which of the Five Precepts is most difficult for you?

Do no harm to anyone.
Take nothing that is not freely given.
Use sexual energy wisely.
Speak truthfully and helpfully.
Keep the Mind clear.

Why don't you think you can keep this Precept? Journal for five minutes or contemplate this question while you are gardening today.

THE MEDITATIVE GARDENER

Renunciation

I've finally renounced buying full-sun perennials because I've finally admitted to myself that I have a partial-shade garden. I still ogle the colorful full-sun flowers at the garden center. New colors and selections come out every year, and I often spot one I'd like to add to my garden. Instead, I now smile, sigh, and bid it goodbye.

Abandoning anything runs counter to our culture of acquisition. Yet the sources of Stress (full-sun flowers that flop in the shade or that barely bloom) must be let go of in order for happiness to arise (shade perennials that perform well in the shade).

Renunciation is a practice of non-Greed. When the Buddha spoke about Renunciation, he suggested giving up behaviors that cause Suffering and Stress, such as those that violate ethical precepts. It can also mean giving up a more seemingly benign habit, such as buying full-sun flowers for a shade garden. The idea is that by refraining from a behavior that causes Suffering, we are laying the ground for the cultivation of wholesome action that will bring happiness.

We might, for example, consider renouncing whatever it is that distracts us from our meditation practice. For me that has meant giving up some evening activities, including going to the movies. A few years ago I realized that as much as I love movies, if I want to meditate in the evening and read a few pages of a Dharma book, I need to have the solitude of being at home. Another thing: I now turn off the computer an hour before bedtime,[11] allowing myself time to sit before I fall asleep.

For you, Renunciation might mean giving up something aesthetically pleasing. A friend complained about the weeds growing in her driveway. I told her I had given up fighting that constant battle in favor of a trim green swath (not necessarily all grass!) along the edge of the driveway.

It's important to realize that when we renounce something we're making a choice—perhaps to disengage from the world for a few minutes or hours in order to restore ourselves in our own gardens. In doing so, we allow both Calm and happiness to arise.

In Renunciation we are, in essence, simplifying. The effects of our actions are not only personal, but familial, communal, and even global. The bumper sticker, "Live simply so that others may simply live" comes from the Voluntary Simplicity movement, which asks us to be aware of how our actions affect other human beings, in our own community and across the country, as well as the planet itself. Can we consume fewer things, waste less energy, and tread more lightly upon the earth so that others may breathe cleaner air, drink unpolluted water? We reap personal benefits from voluntarily renouncing desire, as well. When we are less intent on buying (and earning the money to buy whatever it is), we often find we have more time as well as more money.

THE MEDITATIVE GARDENER

Contemplation on Simplifying

Consider these questions while you are in the garden today.

How might you simplify your gardens or gardening practices?

What would you need to renounce in order to have time for your meditation practice?

Garden Center Contemplation #1

Next time you go to a garden center, renounce buying one thing that you might otherwise buy on impulse.

Take a good look at it. Feel your desire. Notice your Mind pleading.

Then leave whatever it is on the shelf and say, "Good-bye." Send it a wish that it may find a good home and leave the garden center.

Check in with yourself the next day. Can you recall what the object of your desire looked like? Have you sort of forgotten it?

How strong is your desire for it now? Rank your desire on a scale of zero (no desire) to ten (I'm definitely going back to buy it).

If your desire has diminished, notice the difference and contemplate how that happened.

If desire has remained the same or increased, contemplate how that happened.

Wisdom

You can read all the "how-to" books on gardening, and there are many (I know because I have shelves of them), but not until you've dug your hands in the earth will you be a gardener. Only you know your own soils, the microclimates of your yard, and how sun and shade work in your garden. (Then, too, sometimes you are just plain lucky!)

Gardening is an experiential practice. So is meditation. You can learn about meditation from books, but not until you begin sitting yourself will your practice bear fruit, and the fruit of meditation is Wisdom. Making time to attend one meditation retreat each year is invaluable. Reading and studying Dharma books deepens your understanding. Sitting with a weekly group steadies your practice. But meditating daily is the biggest support toward your goal of Wisdom.

The major insights that lead to Wisdom are that every moment is marked by three characteristics: Impermanence, Stress, and Emptiness.

We know Impermanence as a concept. Of course everything changes. But we act as if we don't know it, we seem to be surprised when the garden changes. "I just thinned out the coreopsis three years ago," a friend complained to me, "and now look at it." She pointed to a patch three feet in diameter.

Apparently she expected the coreopsis to stay thinned.

Gardening with perennials is fundamentally an attempt at homeostasis. Homeostasis derives from Latin and means "staying the same."

No two gardens are the same.
No two days are the same in one garden.

Hugh Johnson

When my partner cleared some trees so we could see a swath of sky, a patch of moss that had been hiding in the woods was revealed. I've tried to maintain that moss patch–in nearly full sun–for 15 years. It has not been easy, since moss wants to grow in damp shade. More moss is ceasing than is arising. I am trying to maintain the homeostasis of a permanent moss bed, but when I see more dead moss than green moss I experience the dissatisfaction of Stress.

When we understand that the noun "garden" is a concept, that "garden" is actually a slow-moving verb of ever-changing flowers, plants, conditions, and even soil, then we can glimpse the Emptiness of the garden. Wisdom is at ease with these essential processes of Impermanence, Stress, and Emptiness.

> If we learn to look at a flower in a way that impermanence is revealed to us, when it dies, we will not suffer. Impermanence is more than an idea. It is a practice to help us touch reality.
>
> Thich Nhat Hanh

Wisdom sometimes, but not always, accompanies aging. We all know people to whom "older and wiser" does not apply. More important is to cultivate what Zen master Suzuki Roshi, founder of the Zen Center in San Francisco, called "beginner's mind." By this he meant an openness and even a child-like eagerness toward each experience, each day, moment, breath. Putting aside our preconceptions, judgments, and opinions allows us to notice what our experience actually is.

Thomas Jefferson realized a similar Wisdom 200-plus years ago. He wrote, "Though an old man, I am but a young gardener." This beginner's mind is a great attitude to cultivate for your meditation practice.

Reviewing the insights you have written down in this book can remind you of your experience, help you understand it, and thereby water the seeds of Wisdom.

• • •

Contemplating Wisdom

At the end of your next sitting meditation, drop this wish into the pond of your still reflection: "May I see things as they truly are."

Energy

In the spring I arise with the sun, throw on my gardening clothes, and hurry out to the garden. When I worked a nine-to-five job, this meant I could garden for two hours, shower, and then meditate with my neighbors for an hour before leaving for work at 8:30. Doing my "Stress reduction" (gardening and meditating) before work energized me and made me happy for the rest of the day.

Just as the sun provides Energy, which fuels the growth of plants in the garden, it is important to find your own source of Energy for gardening and meditation practice.

Meditation may appear relaxing; after all, you're just sitting there doing nothing. And some people meditate specifically for the relaxation effect. But as you know, if you've tried to maintain attention on the breath for even five minutes, keeping the focus requires Energy.

Investigating Energy

What motivates you into the garden?

What deters you from getting out to the garden?

What motivates you to meditate?

What deters you from meditating?

Consider these questions the next time you are in the garden or sitting on the cushion.

Patience

Patience. Gardeners know about being patient, whether or not they are good at it. Despite our desires for quick results, that new perennial just planted will not be hurried into lushness. In fact, the perennials we cultivate usually follow this adage:

Impatiens are sometimes called Patient Lucy or the Patience Plant.

> The first year they sleep,
> The second year they creep.
> The third year they leap.

Vegetable gardeners likewise know that when the seed packet says "120 days to maturity," the vegetable will not ripen much sooner than that.

Our meditation practice cannot be rushed along either. Unfortunately it does not come with a note that tells us exactly how long it will be before we can expect to reap the fruits of our practice, but Patience does guarantee that if the seed of Mindfulness is watered and cultivated, our practice bears fruit.

With time and patience,
the mulberry leaf turns into silk.

Chinese proverb

Investigating Impatience

What are you impatient about in your garden?

What are you impatient about in your meditation practice?

List some of the fruits of your meditation practice. Examples might include calmer, less quick to anger, insights about what to do today, less depressed.

Truthfulness

What does the word "organic" actually mean? You'd think it would mean no pesticides, no herbicides, no chemical fertilizers, and no hormones. In fact, small organic farmers go to great lengths to assure the purity of their products. But now that "organic" has become a selling point, other less scrupulous producers want a share of the profits—and today a battle is raging over diluting the meaning of the word "organic."

Have you ever read the word "natural" on a list of ingredients and wondered, "Natural? They must mean 'natural chemicals.'" What is the truth?

The factor behind non-truth is an intention to deceive. If Greed is the motive, the person wants to gain some personal advantage. The word "organic" translates to more sales. If the non-truth is rooted in Aversion, then it becomes a malicious lie. If it is rooted in Delusion, it becomes an irrational lie, an interesting exaggeration, or simply lying for the sake of a joke.

Truth is a commitment to what is real—it is rooted in the soil of reality rather than illusion. Wisdom is the realization of truth. We immediately know when an insight is true, because our Body understands it as well as our Mind. Our Body also knows when we are not being truthful, although the Mind may not want to admit it; likewise we instinctively know when others are not telling the truth.

Our entire practice hinges on whether we think the Buddha was telling us the truth about this path. It is said that in all his previous lives, the Buddha never told a lie.

Investigating Truth Telling

What gets in the way of telling the truth?

What gets in the way of recognizing the truth?

Think about these questions when you are in the garden today.

Lunaria is called Honesty or money plant because of the silver sheen of its seed membranes.

Determination

In early, early spring I have 14 cubic yards of a mixture of composted manure and bark mulch delivered. I long ago resolved to improve the soil of my flower beds. Enriching the soil is something I do not slack on. Distributing this giant pile of compost plus mulch requires continued Determination to haul, haul, haul it in the garden cart.

Doing something which benefits your garden (or yourself), even though you may not want to, requires Determination. On the other hand, refraining from doing something harmful, but which you **do** like to do–such as smoking cigarettes, eating chocolate truffles when you're on a diet, or being catty—also requires Determination.

Determination does not mean grim willpower. I find that I can lighten my grip on the task at hand if I keep in Mind my long-range goal—improved soil in the garden and improved Concentration in my meditation practice. Neither of these goals is going to happen in an hour or even a year, so I may as well enjoy the process.

My meditation practice also requires Determination. It takes Determination to sit regularly. At the beginning of every sit I first remind myself why I am sitting, then I set a resolve, a Determination, about what I intend to do during my sit.

Investigating Determination

Can you think of a gardening project that you don't particularly like? Maybe digging a hole for a shrub? Or dragging the hose around for watering? List any good-for-your-garden projects whose accomplishment requires your Determination.

What are some gardening resolves you have followed through on?

Are there any aspects of meditation you don't particularly like? Sitting regularly, reining in the Mind, or practicing some of the Five Precepts, for instance.

How might you muster Determination without will-power?

List some Determinations you might set at the beginning of your meditation. For example, Concentration, watching the breath, sitting still, becoming aware of thoughts, practicing Loving-Kindness, or doing a Contemplation for the last third of your meditation period.

Loving-Kindness

Visitors to my home take off their jackets and shoes in the mudroom and then step into the living room. The first thing they see is the jungle of houseplants in the adjacent solarium.

"Oh," they say. "It's so beautiful here." And I know their hearts have been opened.

When my brother visited me for the first time at Christmas, he walked directly into the solarium behind the Christmas tree and was "lost" in the 10-foot-by-17-foot room for five minutes.

Allowing yourself to experience deep pleasure and Joy is a foundation for Loving-Kindness.

After practicing some of the Loving-Kindness meditations in this book you may realize that Metta is working in your life as you plant and water the seeds of Good-will and friendliness in your heart. You cultivate these seeds of Loving-Kindness every time you don't turn away from your experience: every time (on or off the cushion) you stay with what is occurring in an open, accepting, friendly way.

In the cherry blossoms' shade
there's no such thing as a stranger.

Issa

Meditation to the Six Directions

May all beings feel happy.
North. South. East. West. Above. Below.
May all beings feel happy.
May all beings be free from Suffering.
North. South. East. West. Above. Below.
May all beings be free from Suffering
May all beings find peace.
North. South. East. West. Above. Below.
May all beings find peace.

Say this meditation today when you are outdoors in the garden.

Equanimity (*Upekkha*)

One day I went to visit Lanice, a 72-year-old Master Gardener. She lived in a house that had been her parents' summer cabin; it was not insulated for New England winters. During the winter her living space shrank to only the living room, heated by a small wood stove where she cooked. As she showed me through her gardens, I could see that she could no longer keep up with her many flower beds. She told me she relied on a 40-something friend to help her out, but that her friend didn't have time to do everything.

Lanice's tended garden was shrinking. She pointed to several untended flower beds, then offered me some closed gentian, which was becoming lost under a spreading mountain laurel bush. She lit up as she showed me her little greenhouse on the south side of the house, which was crammed with unusual houseplants and cuttings rooting in jars. Lanice seemed to accept that her garden would never again be what it once was, and in this acceptance of things as they are she expressed Equanimity.

The spirit of Equanimity is at the heart of the well-known Serenity Prayer,[12] offered at Alcoholics Anonymous and Al-Anon meetings:

> Grant me
>> the serenity to accept the things I cannot change;
>> the courage to change the things I can;
>> and the Wisdom to know the difference.

Equanimity is this acceptance of the things we cannot change—whether our health, our partner, the decisions of our family members, our out-of-control gardens, or the policies of our government. It's important to keep in Mind that Equanimity is acceptance, not indifference.

Equanimity is rooted in the Wisdom that knows the difference between things that can and cannot be changed.

•　•　•

Serenity Meditation

Imagine a still mountain lake, fed by underground springs. On a windless day, this sheltered lake mirrors the surrounding landscape. Look closely at the lake.

Feel the quality of tranquility or serenity

A tree in the surrounding forest may fall, yet this still mountain lake does not tremble.

Explore where this feeling of still water resides in your Body.

Notice what happens to this still water when a thought arises.

Return to the feeling of still water, even if only for a second.

Over time you will become more familiar with this feeling of still water.

Summary

The qualities of Mind which cause Stress—Greed, Aversion, and Delusion—are counteracted by the practice of the Perfections.

Generosity and Renunciation condition the Mind to let go of greedy attachments and desires.

Relaxing into Patience and cultivating Loving-Kindness expand the narrow and aversive Mind.

Wisdom and Equanimity shed light on ignorance and the delusional Mind.

The Parami of Virtue warrants enough attention that we will focus on it separately in the next section, under the Five Precepts. Following the Precepts, which includes observing the Truthfulness of wise speech, is the first step toward reconditioning the Mind. The Buddha repeatedly placed a virtuous life embodied by the Precepts at the beginning of his teachings. The Precepts encourage us to practice non-harming toward other beings and toward ourselves.

The process of consistently redirecting our Minds away from unwholesome thoughts and toward wholesome ones requires Determination and the Energy to follow through with our intentions.

One thing you need to remember and understand is that you cannot leave the Mind alone. It needs to be watched consistently. If you do not look after your garden it will overgrow with weeds. If you do not watch your Mind, defilements will grow and multiply. The Mind does not belong to you but you are responsible for it.

U Tejaniya

The Two Piles Investigation

The Mindfulness we propagate in meditation can alert us to the different Feeling tones between wholesome and unwholesome Mind states, skillful and unskillful actions, and wise speech and harmful speech.

Turning the Mind away from little unwholesome thoughts and onto wholesome thoughts is like pulling annual weeds before they go to seed. Chickweed, purslane, smartweed, and pigweed are examples of weeds that can be virtually eliminated by persistent weeding in one season.

One of my hillside flower beds used to have chickweed (*Cerastium vulgatum*) around the lower edge. Since chickweed is an inconspicuous little creeper that flowers underneath the snow, I had to pull it before it went to seed at crocus time. A couple of years ago, I noticed, "Oh yeah. I used to have chickweed in this garden, but now it's gone."

As the sign beside my vegetable garden says, "Weed 'em and reap."

As you go through your daily life, divide your thoughts and actions into two piles.

One heap is labeled "Perfections." The other is labeled "Everything else."

Into the "Perfections" category, place all your thoughts and actions of Generosity, Virtue, Renunciation, Wisdom, Energy, Patience, Truthfulness, Determination, Loving-Kindness, and Equanimity.

Place all your other thoughts and actions into the pile labeled "Everything else."

Practice for an hour, a day, or a week.

Reflect on this while you are in your garden.

THE FIVE PRECEPTS[13]

OUR ENTIRE SPIRITUAL PATH SPROUTS from a root system of ethics. Nourishing the healthy roots of a virtuous life enables us to continue walking our walk without stumbling on the stones of regret or remorse. The Five Precepts that ground our practice support ethical relationships to ourselves and to all other beings.

> I undertake the Precept to refrain from destroying living creatures.
> I undertake the Precept to refrain from taking that which is not offered.
> I undertake the Precept to refrain from sexual misconduct.
> I undertake the Precept to refrain from harmful speech.
> I undertake the Precept to refrain from intoxicants that can lead to carelessness.

Our culture puts pleasure on a pedestal, but no one can lead a life where only pleasant things happen—not even Prince Siddhartha who became the Buddha, not even Jesus who became the Christ, not Moses, and not Mohammed.

I came of age during the sexual revolution when Abbie Hoffman wrote *Steal This Book*. Most of my friends smoked pot while we listened to the lamenting lyrics of folk songs and to Motown and rock 'n roll. It was the era of Vietnam and I lived in a conservative state where almost everyone I knew supported the war. Morality seemed so old-fashioned.

After finishing a Master's degree program in the early '70s, I shared a house with twelve of my classmates, including a former boyfriend. After I had an abortion, he started sharing his bed with another classmate. To compensate, I had some casual sexual partners. I was sprouting avocado pits on one kitchen window sill and someone else was starting marijuana seeds in the other window. Smoking dope made me paranoid and sleepy; I took up smoking cigarettes to relieve my tremendous anxiety. We all saved money on groceries by stealing toilet paper from our alma mater. I very soon fell into a black pit of depression.

Thanks to a mentor, I began meditating, which, after several months, relieved both the anxiety and the depression. Still I felt vulnerable for the next few years, and there were some lessons, particularly about relationships, that took me several years to learn.

As a result of emotional Suffering, I eventually demoted certain pleasures to second place. My peace of Mind turned out to be more important than sex, drugs, and rock 'n roll.

Suffering is the impetus that drives many of us toward a spiritual path. The motivation to put our lives in order does not come from judging as bad or evil actions that at one time might have brought pleasure. Rather, because those pleasure-seeking actions have led to mental pain or emotional Suffering, we eventually decide to just stop. Our spiritual path is an experiential path. Living an ethical life puts the conscience at ease and lays the foundation for a wiser life.

The Five Precepts are guidelines for laypeople. They are not commandments. Nor are they imposed by an outside authority. Each person has to search for her own relationship to each Precept.

Many Buddhists recite these Precepts every day. Some people choose only the Precepts they can truly live with. You might "try on" a difficult Precept for a day and see how it feels. Over an extended period of time, even the more rigorous Precepts may become easier.

THE MEDITATIVE GARDENER

I vow to refrain from harming living creatures.

Every summer I go out to the vegetable garden in July and find leafless tomato plants. That clue tells me to look very carefully for the big but well-camouflaged green tomato hornworm.

If the hornworm has raised white dots on its back, I know that a parasitic wasp has laid its eggs on the hornworm and that the caterpillar's days are numbered. The hornworm is the larval form of the Five-Spotted Hawkmoth. But what to do about those big green dudes, without the spots, that are seriously munching tomato foliage?

I cannot bear to squish the caterpillars, which cling to tomato plants like Velcro. For many years, I carefully pulled them off with my fingers and put them in a jar of soapy water. Eventually I couldn't even bear to drown them. Now I deport them far enough into the woods where they will not be able to crawl to one of their host plants—tomatoes or sweet-scented *Nicotiana*, which volunteers in abundance near the vegetable garden.

This Precept of refraining from destroying living creatures encourages us to develop the wholesome habit of harmlessness, but as a gardener, you may have some serious questions to ponder in your own heart.

To use pesticides or to pick bugs off plants? To flick the pests into soapy water or deport them? To swat a mosquito or brush it away? What do you do about the chipmunk that eats your tulip bulbs? How do you feel about the deer that eat every shrub and perennial in your yard? What about accidentally halving an earthworm?

How about using bone or blood meal to feed spring bulbs? Blood meal is an excellent source of nitrogen, but consider where it comes from.

My sweetie, angered by the disappearance of tulips from our bulb garden, set his sights on the chipmunks that live in a nearby stone wall. He once caught them in a Hav-a-Heart trap and deported them to Swamp Road, a woodsy road with no homes nearby. However, transporting wild animals turned out to be illegal in our area. Besides, the survival rate of transplanted chipmunks is very low.

Searching for an alternative, I planted tulips in plastic pots in the ground. I also tried planting the bulbs on a bed of crushed oyster shells on the theory that the sharp edges would hurt tender chipmunk noses and deter them. I added cedar shavings, hoping that the strong smell would repel chipmunks. I forced tulips by planting them in pots and kept them in my basement until early spring. None of these alternatives worked very well. So I decided to treat tulips as annuals—buy them at half price in November and plant them every year. Then one spring none came up; apparently the tulips had made a nice winter feast for a chipmunk family. Finally, I renounced planting tulips altogether and just enjoyed watching the chipmunks cavorting in my flower beds. So far, this is the decision that produces the least Stress.

Harmlessness hinges on intention. According to Buddhist texts, intending to kill something produces more karmic consequences than accidentally harming it. Sometimes when pests are rampant, you may decide to take the karma upon yourself anyway. Ridding a meditation center of ants, flies, or roaches may enable the center to stay open rather than have the health department close it down, for example. Or what about removing an embedded (and potentially disease-carrying) tick from your arm and drowning it so that it does not infect others? What's the difference in the feel of intended harm ("I'm going to get you") and the accidental harm of cutting an earthworm with your trowel? Noticing how harming feels to you expands your understanding of this Precept.

In Buddhist cosmology, plants, although sensitive, are not considered sentient beings because they do not have consciousness.

Contemplation on the Stages of a Butterfly[14]

Is there a butterfly farm near you? Go visit it. Sit on a bench in the butterfly house and notice how you feel.

Even if you can't go to a butterfly farm today, consider the stages of a butterfly's life.

Imagine a beautiful butterfly, in as much detail as you can, flitting from flower to flower in your garden or landing on its favorite flower.

Imagine butterflies mating, and then the female laying eggs on a host plant. Imagine finding the tiny red specks on the underside of leaves.

See those eggs hatching into tiny, hungry larvae, which immediately begin to eat the host plant. Over the course of several days, the larval caterpillars become larger and larger.

When one of those caterpillars is big and full, it begins to form a chrysalis. It renounces the world of caterpillar desire and goes into seclusion.

Days or weeks or months later, the pupa shell starts cracking. In your Mind's eye watch a butterfly being born. Then see it perch on the host plant for an hour or so to slowly pump blood into its wings and let them dry out.

Finally the new butterfly flaps its wings, rises into the air, and begins to soar, flitting from plant to plant in your garden.

Notice your feelings toward this sentient being.

As a child I learned to swat flies and mosquitoes without a second thought. I even felt a certain glee at the thought of contributing to their eradication.

One day, thirty years later, after ending my meditation with the wish that all beings would feel safe, peaceful, and free from Suffering, I realized I could no longer step on an ant in the kitchen. Something had happened. That was the beginning of deporting bugs from my house to the great outdoors—ants, wasps, ladybugs, or spiders. Now I really do enjoy liberating the creatures I find inside my home and sending them back to their native country where they can be free to live their own lives.

While on a solo retreat at a primitive campsite on a lake, I realized the lean-to had cockroaches. The park ranger came by and encouraged me to use the giant can of roach-killer, which stood on a high shelf in the lean-to. Then she saw my Buddha statue sitting on the picnic table beside a bouquet of wildflowers in a plastic cup. "Oh, maybe I shouldn't say that to you," she said.

I smiled.

Later I sprayed the floor of the lean-to with the roach-killer. It smelled so familiar. Then I realized it smelled like motel bathrooms and airport bathrooms. I did smash some cockroaches as they skittered away. I tried to feel that I was helping the campers who would follow me, but in truth I felt rather ill.

Eventually I decided not to return to that campsite with the beautiful beach. I just could not kill any more cockroaches.

Where there are humans
You'll find flies,
and Buddhas.

Basho

125

Loving–Kindness Meditation toward Bugs

Do you have any favorite insects? Butterflies, for instance? I once watched a dragonfly breathe, so I love dragonflies, damselflies, and darning needles. Fireflies and water striders are fun to watch.

Is there some insect you feel friendly toward? Perhaps the woolly bear,[15] which predicts winter, or crickets, whose chirping indicates deep summer. Perhaps one of the beneficials, such as ladybugs or lacewings, which eat aphids, white flies, and spider mites.

What bug do you feel neutral toward? Leafhoppers, daddy long-legs, walking sticks, or praying mantises?

Think about an insect you do not like. Don't choose your worst enemy; choose one that displeases you only a little. Maybe ants are okay outdoors (where they lick peonies open) but you do not like them in your house; or choose bees (if you are not allergic to them), which do good work and produce honey but have a sting.

Imagine your favorite insect and say your Loving-Kindness phrases to it. "May you feel safe. May you feel happy. May you feel strong. May you feel peaceful."

Imagine an insect you feel friendly toward and say your Loving-Kindness phrases to it.

Imagine your neutral insect and say your Loving-Kindness phrases to it.

Imagine an insect that irritates you and say your Loving-Kindness phrases to it.

"May all beings be free from Suffering. May all beings feel happy."

Mosquito Meditation

My forester friend, Lynn Levine, works in the woods and has taught herself not to swat mosquitoes. She says this requires setting a Determination to respond to a mosquito buzz as she would any other slightly annoying noise, such as a lawn-mower—and not to swat. Part of her technique is to wear mosquito-appropriate clothing; even on a hot summer day, she wears long sleeves and long pants when she's visiting the home of mosquitoes.

The next time mosquitoes are buzzing around you, listen. Notice the sound and label it pleasant, unpleasant, or neutral. Notice your hand. Notice your mood. Pay close attention to where the Mind goes in response to the sound.

Notice the sensations of a mosquito landing on your skin. Label that sensation pleasant, unpleasant or neutral. Notice where the Mind goes as soon as you feel a mosquito on your skin. Notice where your hands go.

Notice any tensing of the Body. Is it possible to relax? Is there any difference in your Stress level when the Body relaxes? Pay close attention to what is happening in the Mind and in the Body.

If a mosquito does bite you, continue to notice the bite area off and on through-out the day and evening. Notice the sensations and notice what the Mind is doing.

How does the mosquito bite feel the next morning?

I vow to refrain from taking that which is not offered.

At the foot of the private road that I share with several neighbors, I plant daffodils to cheer us up in the early spring. My neighbors all enjoy this bright spot and many of them have thanked me repeatedly. One April day as I turned onto our road, I noticed that the daffodils had been picked. Some passer-by had taken home a yellow bouquet.

This Precept of refraining from taking what is not offered encourages us to develop the wholesome habit of honesty. It's another way to practice non-harming—toward our community and toward ourselves.

When walking through a botanical garden, have you ever been tempted to pick a seed head of some exotic lovely plant? How about digging up plants on the side of the road? How about picking the fruit off a neighbor's tree that branches into your yard? Have you ever snuck seeds or plants from foreign countries through customs?

Sometimes Nature's resources are mined as if the goal is to take everything now (or within the next fifty years). Even sustainable resources that could be used in perpetuity, such as forests, water, and soil, are sometimes used wastefully, as if there's an infinite supply.

While some landscapes, such as the woodlands of the eastern United States, can rebound fairly quickly, other habitats, such as the Plains or the desert, take decades

or even centuries to rebuild from overgrazing, over-cutting, hard-rock mining, and other such assaults.

If we think of Nature as a resource to be used for the benefit of all, does such "mining" of Nature constitute taking what is not offered? Preserving the environment as the wealth we hold in common applies even to our gardens, tiny though they may be compared to scale of agribusiness.

To supplement our own gardens, we buy locally at farmers' markets; this supports local farms and cuts down on the resources required to transport fruits and vegetables thousands of miles to area supermarkets.

As vegetable gardeners, we are practicing sustainable agriculture because we want to be able to harvest our gardens for many years. For this reason, we enrich the soil each year with compost and organic fertilizers; we rotate crops, and avoid pesticides that will remain in the environment for years to come. If we want to practice ethical gardening, we need to look deeply into our gardening practices and ask ourselves whether what we are doing today will cost or benefit future generations.

A farmer should live as though he were going to die tomorrow; but he should farm as though he were going to live forever.

East Anglia proverb

Reflecting on the Life Cycle of Chemicals

While sitting on his patio, my nephew noticed yellow-jackets buzzing around his one-year-old son, so my nephew sprayed the yellow-jackets' nest with wasp and hornet killer. Then his bee-eating dog, a chocolate Labrador retriever, ate the dead yellow-jackets.

"So let me get this straight," I said. "Your dog just ate poisoned bees."

"Uh-huh," he said. "He's a dog."

Do you use any chemical fertilizers, pesticides, or herbicides?

What is your rationale for using these?

As you walk around your gardens today, consider the effects of fertilizers, pesticides, and herbicides. What happens to them after the lawn is green or the bug or weed is dead? The chemicals don't just disappear. Where do they go?

Contemplation on Taking What is Not Offered

Have you taken something without it being offered to you? What?

What was your rationale for this action?

If one of your thoughts was "Oh, they won't mind," or "Oh, they won't notice," do you know this to be true?

Who does mind? Who is noticing?

I vow to refrain from sexual misconduct.

> I used to love my garden
> but now my love is dead.
> I found a bachelor's button
> in black-eyed Susan's bed.[16]

Whether or not we've been affected by infidelity, we can recognize the Suffering engendered as a result of betrayal in sexual relationships.

Pro-*misc*-uous comes from the same root as *misc*-ellaneous and "mixed up." In sexual misconduct, many things—priorities, loyalties, vows—get mixed up. While pleasure predominates, at least part of the time, if you stand back, you can weigh how much time is spent in pleasure and how much time is spent in heartache, longing, fantasizing, distress, or some other form of Stress. Have you ever sacrificed your own well-being for momentary pleasure?

I was a late bloomer. I met my sweetheart when I was past forty. I had dated for twenty years, which gave me plenty of time to practice sexual misconduct and receive its effects.

This Precept can point us beyond outright sexual misconduct to include our inner thoughts. When we relate to other people as sexual objects or as a means to our own ends, we are using them for what we can get from them—whether it's sex, power, money, or status.

Objectifying another person can be very subtle. In the classic Hollywood movie, a man croons to a young woman (never a middle-aged or an older woman), "You're so pretty" as code to mean "I want to go to bed with you." Even though the sentence sounds like a compliment, it's actually about what the speaker wants from the object he is looking at. "You're so pretty" is a "You" statement which, translated to an "I" statement, would say something like, "I feel so good and happy and sexy when I look at you."

All the -isms—sexism, racism, ageism, fat-ism—respond to the way people look. They can collectively be called "rankism" because in our Minds we are ranking people above or below us. Rather than seeing people as objects, how can we respond directly heart to heart?

This Precept of using our sexual energy wisely encourages us to relate harmlessly to one another by being trustworthy and responsible.

Single people with no particular loyalties may have to delve deeply into this Precept to determine their own relationship to it. How can you practice not treating another person as an object? How can you cause the least harm to everyone involved? How can you practice wise speech when it's time to break off a liaison?

In Roman times, basil was thought to stimulate sensuality.[17]

Sexual Misconduct Inquiry

Have you been affected by someone's sexual misconduct?
Today while you are in the garden, remember how that felt.
Can you resolve to yourself not to do that to someone else?

Have you ever been sexually foolish or inappropriate?
How did that feel at the time? How do you feel about it now?

THE MEDITATIVE GARDENER

I vow to refrain from harmful speech.

Not long ago, while driving a truck loaded with bark mulch, I braked sharply for a five-way intersection at the bottom of a steep hill. The momentum of the heavier-than-usual load carried me farther forward into the intersection than I would have liked. On the road to my left, a woman leaned out her car window and screamed at me.

I was stunned, hurt, and furious. What right had she to yell at me when I was doing the best I could, given the situation? I wanted to shout back at her. I also wanted to explain my action and to let her know how inappropriate her road rage was. I noted my anger, irritation, and desire for self-defense. She had thrown a verbal hot potato at me and I recognized the impulse to toss it right back at her (as I was already doing in my Mind). Instead, I stopped, took a breath, and politely waved at her to take her turn and continue through the intersection.

When you are on the receiving end of harsh speech, it can be very difficult to weather the blame that's hurled at you. There's an old maxim: "Don't throw stones in your garden," meaning "Don't retaliate." As a gardener in New England's rocky soil, I throw hundreds of rocks out of the garden, but I now try to be careful about verbal hot potatoes. If you toss one at someone, chances are it will be flung right back at you. If you catch one, it takes strong Determination to hold onto it, or sidestep it, all the time noting, "Anger. Anger. Anger (or whatever your label might be)."

When we take the Precept to refrain from harmful speech, we are setting the intention not only to abstain from hurling verbal abuses or insults, but to practice wise speech. This Precept encourages us to develop the wholesome habit of friendliness by speaking in a way that is easy to listen to. Speaking skillfully has six qualities. It should be truthful, harmonious, comforting, useful, worth taking to heart, and timely.

Taking time—whether before or after you utter something—to determine whether what you are saying meets all six of these requirements can be very instructive. Truthfulness alone is not enough reason to say something. We all know that speech can be hurtful, although true, just as it can be comforting but deceitful.

The other side of the wise speech coin is the practice of right listening. Half-listening to someone while thinking about what you want to say next is not skillfull listening.

Do you garden with family or friends or in a community garden? What do you usually talk about? Consider setting some of your garden time or a space in your garden aside as a sanctuary in which you can practice skillful speech.

Gardening with a Friend Meditation

Ask a meditation friend to come help you in your garden. Even if she has not the slightest interest in helping you weed, set an intention between the two of you to speak skillfully for 15 or 30 minutes. Try to make your conversation kind, useful, beneficial; and true.

Then review the awkwardnesses and difficulties you had in following through on your intention.

•   •   •

Investigating the Six Elements of Wise Speech

What's a recent example in your own life of failing to speak skillfully? Think of something you said that you regret.

Which element of skillful speech was lacking in your example?
> *truthful*
> *harmonious*
> *comforting*
> *useful*
> *worth taking to heart*
> *timely*

I vow to refrain from intoxicating drinks and drugs that lead to carelessness.

> We are here and it is now. Further than that all human knowledge is moonshine.
>
> H. L. Mencken

This Precept encourages us to stop watering the roots of Delusion.

When we finally get around to setting an intention to wake up from Delusion, then we do not want to take the chance of missing one moment because we are "under the influence" of an enchanting substance.

The word "toxic" lies in the middle of the word "intoxicating." "Toxic" sounds dangerous, but "intoxicating" sounds like fun. The enormous gap between the two words reveals how subtle Delusion can be. Intoxication is an enchantment, and while we are enchanted we usually don't notice the toxicity of which we are partaking; we're like Snow White accepting the apple.

We want to ingest healthy things for the Body and Mind. We would not knowingly ingest toxins; nor would we knowingly use toxins to nourish our plants or plant our gardens on toxic soil, because we know that poisons work their way from the earth into the plants, fruit or vegetable, and onto our plates and into our bodies. What's more, every human being alive already carries a burden of heavy metals in her Body.[18]

When I saw hundreds of people taking this Precept, of refraining from intoxicants, at a retreat with the Vietnamese monk and teacher Thich Nhat Hanh, I was astounded because I couldn't yet take the Precept myself. I had already given up hard liquor because I didn't really enjoy the taste. I could never remember the names of wines, so I assumed that I wasn't really interested in wine and I had stopped drinking it. That left beer. How could I deprive my German genes of beer? I loved tasting the beers of the countries I traveled to. Due to occasional cleansing diets, I usually drank non-alcoholic beer (which is in fact alcoholic, but below the half-percent legal standard).

But watching my mother die of alcoholism pushed me over the edge of any doubt about this Precept. She had stopped drinking four weeks before she died. Soon after that, I simply stopped drinking, too, recognizing that it was time.

We all have friends who are alcoholics or users. Consider taking a Bodhisattva[19] vow and abstaining from intoxicants for the benefit of your friend, even if it's only for one evening while you are in her company.

Investigating Your Favorite Avenues of Escape

List your favorite avenues of escape. Gardening may be at the top of the list, which could also include activities such as shopping, cell-phoning or texting, reading, doing crossword puzzles or Sudoku, sewing, watching TV, listening to the news, playing computer games, surfing the internet, checking your email, gambling, or playing Bingo. Substances might include chocolate, sugar, coffee, or food in general, as well as alcohol, tobacco, marijuana, or other intoxicants.

List your favorite escapes:

What are you escaping from?

Is this escape a habit you want to feed?

List the pleasant side effects of intoxication.

Are there any unpleasant side effects?

Is there another way to achieve the pleasant side effects?

Summary

The Five Precepts guide us toward a virtuous life in which we recognize that other sentient beings wish to feel happy just as we ourselves do. Our desire to be harmless toward other sentient beings gives us a sense of well-being. By wishing other beings well, we ourselves become recipients of well-being.

Bit by bit, we take the crookedness out of our own behaviors.

I have come to terms with the future. From this day onward I will walk easy on the earth. Plant trees. Kill no living things. Live in harmony with all creatures. I will restore the earth where I am. Use no more of its resources than I need. And listen, listen to what it is telling me.

M. J. Slim Hooey

Investigating the Five Precepts

The Five Precepts are guidelines that call us to Mindfulness.

> Do no harm to anyone.
> Take nothing that is not freely given.
> Use sexual energy wisely.
> Speak truthfully and helpfully.
> Keep the Mind clear.[20]

Which Precept(s) can you commit to today?

It might be assumed that we are always aware of the present, but this is a mirage.

Bhikkhu Bodhi

S O FAR, WE HAVE BEEN planting the Body, Feelings, and Mind in the garden. Despite this, it can be difficult to stay in touch with the thread of Mindfulness while gardening. You notice putting your gloves on, feel the texture as your fingers enter a protected space. The next thing you remember is placing the trowel back on the shelf. What happened in between?

As the writer James Joyce said about his character, Mr. James Duffy, "He lived at a little distance from his body, regarding his own acts with doubtful side-glances. He had an odd autobiographical habit which led him to compose in his Mind from time to time a short sentence about himself containing a subject in the third person and a predicate in the past tense."[21]

Like Mr. Duffy, we all tell ourselves stories about ourselves.

Perhaps the gardening Mind has not been mindful exactly, but are there times when it stops racing around and settles down on one subject like a cow chewing its cud in a pasture?

If mulling-over is a familiar process to you, you can see that the Mind naturally goes to Contemplation in the garden. So let's use this natural bent of the Mind, with its underpinnings of Calm, tranquility, and peace, and apply it to subjects of Contemplation that were recommended by the Buddha.

The next section contains a selection of such Contemplations that you can use in the garden as you commune with your plants and the nature of things as they are.

Yes, the Mind takes a long time, is otherwise occupied than by happiness, and deep breathing.

Mary Oliver

CONTEMPLATIONS

AFTER ALL THIS EFFORT TO catch ourselves thinking, we now begin the Contemplations section. What's the difference between Contemplation and thinking?

A contemplating Mind grazes within a fenced-in meadow, unlike the discursive Mind, which gallops off over the prairie. During Contemplation, the Mind stays on topic. If this sounds like Mindfulness, it is, and in this section we apply Mindfulness to the thinking Mind. The function of these Contemplations is similar to those in some other contemplative spiritual traditions. As we focus the powerful lens of the mindful Mind on one subject at a time, insight (*vipassana*) arises.

Already we've been practicing at least one Contemplation: The traditional Loving-Kindness meditation, with its four phrases (See page 12), is not only a practice that opens the heart, it is a Contemplation. As you repeat the phrases over and over, insight into their meaning arises.

A few years ago, while I was on retreat, a teacher assigned me some of the Contemplations that I am going to offer you. He gave me one Contemplation per week. I loved them.

Giving the Mind something to investigate, such as a Contemplation, can enliven, deepen, and strengthen your meditation practice, particularly if the Mind has lost interest in the Body or Feelings. Of the many possible Contemplations that Buddhist texts offer us, I have selected some that relate to our practices of gardening and of meditation. They are grouped under five categories or lists.

A few words about these selections:

The Contemplations section opens with the Five Daily Recollections. Three of these Contemplations focus on what Buddhists consider the divine messengers: aging, sickness, and death. The Buddha recommended that we frequently contemplate these messengers. As gardeners we know these messengers as the laws of nature. Together with change and karma they comprise the Five Daily Recollections. Practicing these Recollections on a daily basis provides direct insight into our human existence.

The Four Elements Contemplations focus on the very Body that seems as if it must belong to us. Although we know intellectually that "we have a Body but

147

we are not our Body," we slip very easily into identifying with the Body. Every time we say "I am..." hungry, tired, cold, we are acting as if the Body is indeed our self. By contemplating the Four Elements we see that our Body is composed of the very same "elements" or constituents as the flowers and trees in our gardens.

The Five Hindrances hinder our practice, both during meditation and in everyday life.

The Seven Factors for Awakening Contemplations provide the environment for us to wake up moment by moment, and the Divine Abodes Contemplations (which include Loving-Kindness) open our hearts to ourselves and others as we awaken to our true nature.

The Contemplations section ends with the Three Jewels: the Buddha, Dharma, and Sangha. While Mindfulness of Body, Feelings, and Mind can be incorporated into any spiritual practice, taking refuge in the Three Jewels defines a Buddhist. Many people practice both the tradition they grew up in as well as Buddhism. The choice is yours.

By now you've been introduced to many of the Buddhist lists, and perhaps you've wondered: Why all those lists? The lists in this and in previous sections come from a time when the Buddha's teachings were transmitted by word of mouth from generation to generation. The five of this, the three of that, the seven of the other thing sound odd to us, but they were mnemonic devices of an oral tradition, for remembering the teachings before they were written down. Once we become familiar with a particular list, we too may find it easier, for example, to remember what the Three Roots of Stress are because there are three of them. When we can remember at least three or four of the Five Hindrances, we will be on our way to greater awareness of the Mind states that hinder our Mindfulness.

THE FIVE DAILY RECOLLECTIONS[22]

THE GARDEN IS A FINE place to practice the Five Daily Recollections. Usually, these facts of life are contemplated during the last several minutes of a sitting meditation. Chances are, though, you've already practiced some of the Contemplations informally.

> I am of the nature to grow old. Aging is inevitable.
> I am of the nature to become ill. Sickness is unavoidable.
> I am of the nature to die. Death is unavoidable.
> Everything I cherish will change and vanish.
> My actions are the only thing I own.

These phrases may at first seem morbid or pessimistic. Yet have you ever met anyone who did not grow old, become sick, or die? Ignoring the facts of life does not mean they will not happen. Ignoring them leads simply to ignor-ance.

The Five Daily Recollections are based on the events in the life of the Buddha. The prince Siddhartha Gotama grew up in a palace protected and unaware of age, sickness, or death until at age 29 he ordered his charioteer to take him on a tour of the city. There, for the first time, he saw an old person and he became distressed. The next day he went out in the chariot and saw a sick person. The next he saw a dead person lying beside the road. Finally, he saw a wandering ascetic who looked peaceful, despite the aging, sickness, and death around him. How could that be?

Soon after Siddhartha left his family and his palace and took up the life of a wandering ascetic. He wandered for six years before he found the path to enlight-enment under the bodhi tree and became a Buddha—a fully awakened one.

Our society and culture are as pleasure-seeking as the palace in which Prince Siddhartha grew up. Moreover, the pull of Delusion is very strong; extricating ourselves requires tremendous effort. It necessitates shifting our gaze from how we wish things were to "the way things are."

As gardeners we know very well that the flower of a daylily blooms, ages, and dies within the span of a single day. Irises bloom for a few days before their flower bodies wither and brown and curl into an iris fetal position. Daisies last for a week or more before their petals shrivel up. Ornamental trees drop their flower petals on the ground where they lie beautifully in state before composting into the lawn. We gardeners have our fingers on the pulse of life as we watch hundreds of flowers bloom, age, perhaps become sick, and die every gardening season. We know at a visceral level that we human beings also have a life cycle. We, too, are part of the cycle of life.

> We accept the graceful falling
> of mountain cherry blossoms,
> but it is much harder for us
> to fall away from our own
> attachment to the world.
>
> Rengetsu

I am of the nature to grow old. Aging is inevitable.

I discovered gardening when I was twenty-nine. By age fifty-five, my back had started to complain, especially during the spring, when the garden requires the heaviest work—unloading and spreading truckloads of manure in the vegetable plot; unloading more truckloads of mulch, along the wooded edges of the driveway, plus spreading fourteen cubic yards of compost and mulch in the flower beds.

Something had to give. So I hired Sabrina Smith, a 32-year-old single mother, to help me. What was most difficult was admitting that I could no longer maintain the garden alone. This required recognizing the first of the Contemplations, that *I am growing older!*

Chart of Gardening Chores by Age

My friend Fritze Till saw Ruth Stout[23] talking to a garden club in upscale New Canaan, Connecticut, in the 1970s, when Ruth was more than 90. As the still spirited, but now frail nonagenarian sat in front of the group in her worn-out chenille bathrobe, someone asked her, "Where do you store your winter squash?"

Without missing a beat, Ruth quipped, "Under the kitchen table."

As you look back on your gardening life what do you notice? Has anything changed? Are there gardening chores that you can no longer do? That you had to give up as you got older?

Are there gardening chores with which you must now help your grandmother? Mother? Father? Aunt? A neighbor?

Imagine gardening when you are 30, 40, 50, 60, 70, 80, 90, 100.

As you anticipate the future, how long do you expect to garden? As you look at people older than you, what do you notice? Many widows in their 70s move into condos, limiting their gardening to a few pots at the entry or on the balcony.

Check off the chores you expect to be doing at age . . .	30	40	50	60	70	80	90	100
Mowing your lawn								
Hiring someone to mow your lawn								
Eliminating your lawn								
Rototilling your vegetable garden								
Spading your vegetable garden								
Manuring								
Mulching								
Raking leaves								
Leaving the leaves on the flower beds for lasagna gardening								
Letting the wind do the raking								

Check off the chores you expect to be doing at age . . .	30	40	50	60	70	80	90	100

How many hours a day will you spend gardening?
    maximum
    minimum								

Digging holes for shrubs								

Hiring someone to help you
    once in a while
    weekly								

Training younger gardeners								
Weeding								
Dead-heading								
Creating new beds								
Letting beds go								
Using shrubs instead of perennials								
Dividing plants								
Hauling the hose around								
Raising plants from seeds								
Transplanting								
Hoeing								
Pruning your own trees								
Bending over								
Kneeling								
Taking a stool out to the garden								
Protecting your skin								
Sitting on the ground								
Stopping before you're totally worn out								
Using a cane or walking stick								
Pushing a wheelbarrow								
Pulling a garden cart								

Check off the chores you expect to be doing at age . . .	30	40	50	60	70	80	90	100
Downsizing your gardens								
Buying more garden books								
Buying a condo and letting someone else do the yard work								
Living with a relative or in a nursing home								
Giving up gardening altogether								

THE MEDITATIVE GARDENER

Daffodil Contemplation

Think of your favorite spring bulbs—crocuses, daffodils, tulips, or hyacinths, for example.

Recall the life cycle. Imagine the day you first notice green shoots. How do you feel? Remember the day when you see buds. Feel the Joy of the first blooms. Imagine the petals drying up and browning around the edges as the flower grows older. Visualize the day when you notice that the flowers have drooped or lost all their petals. How do you feel?

Eventually as you walk by, you reach out and dead-head the flower. Imagine this, too.

• • •

Vegetable Garden Contemplation

Do you start any seedlings indoors?

Choose your favorite vegetable and imagine the life cycle of this plant—from seed to seedling to hardening off to transplanting. Picture yourself watering it, and then checking on it in the garden. Imagine weeding around it. Remember the first flowers, the first green fruit, the ripening fruit. Visualize yourself picking the fully ripe fruits, more and more of them until the plant begins to brown at the edges. Finally the days become short enough or cool enough that the plant stops producing.

Grandparent Gardener Contemplation

Both my grandmothers grew up on farms and loved gardening even after they moved to town. One grandmother had her leg amputated due to diabetes when she was 71. One day my uncle came home and found her, out of her wheelchair, sitting in the dirt of the vegetable garden, weeding.

My other grandmother walked with a cane beginning in her 50s and was completely hobbled by arthritis all through her 60s and 70s. Then she inched along using a walker until she died at 84. Every time I visited her, she would take me on a tour of the flowerbed surrounding her house and use her cane (laying it across her walker) to point at her loveliest flowers.

My mother was the sort of gardener who loved easy-care plastic flowers. As a teenager I was embarrassed by the plastic tulips that "grew" all summer in a flower bed in the front lawn. Plastic geraniums in pots adorned her front step throughout the year.

Gardening is apparently a skipped-generation gene in my family.

Think of a relative—a parent, grandparent, or other family member—or a friend from whom you inherited your gardening "gene."

Recall the span of her gardening life, and (if you know) how it changed over the years.

If she is still alive, visualize her and say, "I am of the nature to grow old. Aging is inevitable." If she has already departed think of her near the end of her gardening life and say, "I am of the nature to grow old. I cannot avoid aging."

Today while you are in the garden, contemplate this person, her life span, and your life span as you repeat, "I am of the nature to grow old. Aging is inevitable."

I am of the nature to become ill. Sickness is inevitable.

Perhaps because my father grew up as a Christian Scientist, this reflection has been the most difficult for me. Telling myself that I will become ill seems so pessimistic. I was brought up to believe in Mind over matter, even though I was extremely asthmatic as a child. My father thought my multiple allergies to his horses, barns, and hayfields were all in my Mind, but every six weeks I became bedridden for a week. From age five until I graduated from high school, I became ill frequently.

I am still prone to respiratory problems. My gardening friend, Paul Gustafson, is sure that I garden because digging around in a flower bed frequently requires me to have my nose close to plants and the pure oxygen they produce.

Garden plants are subject to diseases, too. Powdery mildew can afflict phlox, lilacs, some roses, fruit trees, begonias, and African violets. Tomato plants wilt or get brown spot. The list of plant diseases goes on: viruses, lesions, stem rots, galls—and then there are the bugs.

My houseplants spend their summer vacation outdoors. When I bring them inside in September, they are so green, leafy, and strong. Yet, no matter how particular I am about cleaning them, I discover some "bug" a couple of months later; aphids, whiteflies, spider mites, and scale love the warm, well-watered condition of the solarium where the houseplants live during the winter.

Thinking of illness as a dis-ease of the Body makes more sense to me, and so I have changed the word of this Contemplation accordingly. "I am of the nature to have dis-ease. Dis-ease is unavoidable."

Illness Investigation

Are you prone to particular illnesses?

Do you have any chronic pain?

What diseases or bugs bother your plants?

Dis-ease Contemplation

While you are in the garden today, contemplate whichever of the following sentences make the most sense to you.

"I am of the nature to become ill."

"I am of the nature to have dis-ease."

"I am of the nature to become blemished."

"I am of the nature to become sun damaged."

"I am of the nature to have viruses."

"I am of the nature to have 'bugs.'"

"I am of the nature to wilt."

"I am of the nature to have brown spots."

"I am of the nature to wither."

"I am of the nature to become blighted."

"I am of the nature to have dis-ease."

"Dis-ease is unavoidable."

"Sickness is unavoidable."

"Illness is unavoidable."

I am of the nature to die. Death is unavoidable

The first frost kills those annuals that kept me smiling all summer. I go around the flower beds and pull up the wilted bodies of Impatiens, Begonias, basil, and tomatoes, and I sigh as I haul their corpses to the compost pile. Geraniums can usually survive the first light frost, but they do stop flowering. They hold on until a killing frost takes them a week or a month later.

This process has informed my personal decision about advance directives and whether when the "first frost" falls on me I want to continue receiving nutrition and hydration.

Death comes to each and every thing we know, including our precious selves, even if we don't want to think about it.

As gardeners we are face to face with death every day that we are in the garden, whether it's plants, insects, or just a dying blossom. We know that one of these days, we ourselves will be pushing up daisies.

Compost Pile Contemplation

Pull up a lawn chair and sit in front of your compost pile. With your eyes open, look at the compost pile, and repeat these phrases to yourself:

"I am of the nature to die. Death is unavoidable."

Think about the composition of your compost pile.

"I am of the nature to die. Death is unavoidable."

Think about the life cycles of the contents of the pile.

"I am of the nature to die. Death us unavoidable."

The compost pile is a site of transformation, taking what has been cast off and returning it to the garden. It's not just garbage, after all.

The distillation of any philosophy of composting has some connection with the positive concept of waste and death. The contribution that mortality makes to civilization is the equivalent of what composting contributes to a garden.

We are all candidates for composting. So we cannot approach the compost heap without a feeling of connection.

Stanley Kunitz

Plant Marker Contemplation

Sometimes when I'm planting a new perennial, I dig up a white plastic plant marker. I read it and think, "Oh, yeah. That plant. Gone now. It didn't survive in this spot." That plant, which I enjoyed and for which I had high hopes, died.

I have heard of someone who collects the plant markers of departed plants, gathering them like little white plastic tombstones.

> As you walk through your garden today, consider all the plants you have planted that have not survived.
> Say to yourself, "I am of the nature to die. Death is unavoidable."

* * *

Walking Meditation on Death

Every day I make at least one trip to the compost pile, which is the graveyard for my plants and vegetables.

> Today as you walk around your garden, perhaps walking to the compost pile occasionally, think about walking toward your own grave.

Everything I cherish will change and vanish.

I usually begin my period of meditation by reviewing the things I'm grateful for. These are people, places, events, situations, and material objects that I cherish. I also write a gratitude e-mail to a Dharma buddy every day. Yet even by the time I write about what has made me the most happy that day, the event or situation has already changed and usually vanished.

This daily recollection that everything is impermanent begins to sink in when we train our attention on the fact that, yes, everything I have cherished has also changed. Many of those things have also vanished.

After my partner's mother died, I asked for and received most of her gardening tools and statues. She had a narrow trowel with a wooden handle that fit perfectly into my hand. I loved it. Then one spring the handle rotted off. I felt bereft. I kept the trowel blade for a year, thinking I would have someone make me a new handle, but finally I had to admit that this tool I cherished had changed beyond repair. The handle was already rotting into the earth; eventually the blade vanished into the trash.

The Changing Garden Contemplation

When my sister's neighbor, Jessie King, an avid gardener, was selling her house, she felt she needed to plant just a few more flowers in her already beautiful gardens. The people who bought her house had two small boys. Within a couple of years, those beautiful gardens had disappeared.

> *As you stand in the garden today, say to yourself, "Everything I cherish will change and vanish."*
>
> *Think of how the seasons roll through your garden. What does it look like in early spring, spring, late spring, early summer, summer, late summer, early fall, fall, and winter?*
>
> *Say to yourself, "Everything I hold dear will disappear."*
>
> *What do you cherish about your garden?*
>
> *What will this garden look like after you create your dream garden?*
>
> *Say to yourself, "Everything I hold dear will disappear."*
>
> *What will your garden look like after you sell your house?*
>
> *Say to yourself, "Everything I cherish will change and vanish."*
>
> *Practice this Contemplation for the entire time you are in the garden today.*

I am the owner of my actions. I am the heir of my actions.

"Plant a carrot, get a carrot, not a Brussels sprout" sings a line from a song in *The Fantasticks*. The same is true of our actions. If we plant irritation today, we will harvest more irritation an hour from now or tomorrow or next week. If we plant desire, we soon find ourselves heading to the refrigerator or the store or toward people we want to be with, perhaps with the ease of dialing a cell phone or instant messaging.

The seeds of irritation, desire, Aversion, Craving, and Delusion are part of the human condition. Some of these seeds were watered more than others during childhood and by now have become dear and trusted, yet toxic, friends.

Since "the apple doesn't fall far from the tree," we may have inherited Greed, Aversion, or Delusion from one of our parents. My cousin tells the story of how our grandfather, who died long before we were born, accidentally broke my aunt's nose when he slapped her. I can trace the roots of my own Aversion to my father and back to this grandfather.

In English, the word "karma" has come to mean fate or retribution. In Buddhist cosmology, "karma" means something closer to "habit." When the Tibetan teacher Chogyam Trungpa Rinpoche[24] was asked, "What is reborn?" he famously said, "Our bad habits."

The seed of God is in us. If you are an intelligent and hard-working farmer, it will thrive and grow up into God, whose seed it is, and its fruits will be God-fruits. Pear seeds grow into pear trees, nut seeds grow into nut trees, and God seeds grow into God.

Meister Eckhart

THE MEDITATIVE GARDENER

Watering the seeds of anger creates more anger. Watering the seeds of Greed creates more Greed—the feeling of never having enough. Watering the seeds of Delusion creates more ignorance.

The Christian version of karma is phrased as "Evil begets evil." Moving this equation into daily life, we could say, "Impatience begets impatience." "Desire begets desire." "Irritation begets irritation." On the positive side, Loving-Kindness begets Loving-Kindness, as you may have noticed if you've practiced Metta for awhile, particularly toward someone you have a grudge against.

Sprouting Compost Contemplation

I really like it when money plant (*Lunaria*), feverfew, and columbine sprout in my compost. For years, I threw everything into the compost. Then I realized I was also recycling chickweeds, smartweeds, and other nuisances. Now I toss weeds into the woods.

My gardening mentor, Ruth Marx, has what she calls a "dry and die" pile for the weeds she doesn't want to proliferate in the compost.

Contemplate these questions today while you are in the garden:

What sprouts in your compost pile?

How do you think it got there?

What are some of your "bad habits"?

How do you water the seeds of your "bad habits"?

THE MEDITATIVE GARDENER

Summary

I have been contemplating the Five Daily Recollections almost every day for the past few years and I still find them rich enough to hold my interest. I often recite all five, giving one or two minutes to each. Sometimes, toward the end of my meditation period I will focus on one recollection and spend five or twenty-five minutes on it alone.

· · ·

Five Daily Recollections Investigation

Which of the Recollections is the most difficult for you?

I am of the nature to grow old. Aging is inevitable.

I am of the nature to become ill. Sickness is unavoidable.

I am of the nature to die. Death is unavoidable.

Everything I cherish will change and vanish.

My actions are the only thing I own.

THE FOUR ELEMENTS

WHEN I FIRST LEARNED OF the Four Elements—Earth, Water, Air, and Fire—in Buddhism, I thought, "How quaint." But what I really meant was, "How medieval!" The Four Elements brought to Mind astrology and other such New Age practices, which I considered of interest in a symbolic way, but how could this ancient way of seeing the world be relevant to meditation?

Then, on a retreat, a meditation teacher assigned everyone to take a walk and spend an hour doing a Four Elements meditation.

The material world, including our bodies and our gardens, *is* constituted of the Four so-called Elements, I quickly realized. Just as we learned in eighth grade science, matter is either solid, liquid or gas. Earth, Water, Air. These material forms are transmuted from one to the other by heat (Fire) or by the lack of heat. A solid such as ice turns into a liquid (Water) and then into gas (steam) when heat is applied.

> We come from the earth.
> We return to the earth.
> And in between we garden.
>
> Anonymous

Earth embodies the qualities of solidity and extension, hardness, and stiffness. Trees and their solid trunks and extended branches have the qualities of Earth. Our own limbs also have this quality of extension and stability. The Earth elements of the Body are considered to be bones, teeth, and nails.

Water has the qualities of liquidity and cohesion–dewdrops, puddles, a stream. Water can trickle, flow, or congeal. We know the human Body is 70 percent water. The Water elements of the Body include saliva, blood, sweat, tears, lymph, and pus.

Air is gaseous and has the quality of movement and change. Breath is the Air element in the Body.

One of Fire's qualities is temperature—both heat and lack of heat. The Body's normal temperature of 98.6 degrees Fahrenheit is one representation of Fire, as is a warm heart. The heat of our Body composts the food we eat. Fire, or heat, ripens and lightens. Other Fire qualities are energy and destruction. If we look very closely, we can see that the heat of the Body is composting the Body itself.

This body comes into being as a result
of various causes and depends on the
four elements for its existence. It grows
and comes to fruition of different kinds,
just like a tree.

Ajahn Chah

Four Elements Walking Meditation[25]

As you walk around your garden, find a tree to hug. Feel the solidity of the Earth element under your feet and in your arms. Look up into the branches. Notice how their extension through Air is due to the quality of solidity. Notice the solidity and extension of your own Body, your own personal Earth element.

As you continue to walk around your garden, notice the quality of Air. Air comes in through your nose, but it also brushes your skin. If a breeze is blowing, stop and feel the movement aspect of Air into and around the Body.

Now go to the Water element in your garden, whether that is a pond or a bird-bath, a mud puddle or the dew on the grass, a drop of rain or a drop of water from the hose. Feel a drop of water. Play with it. Make a mud pie and notice the cohesive quality of water. Reflect on the cohesive property of water in your Body. Swallow.

If the sun is out, feel its heat as the Fire element. Otherwise, notice the lack of heat. Notice the heat or coolness of your Body.

As you continue to walk around your garden today, name the primary element of each object, each plant you see.

Four Elements Eating Meditation

Begin your meal by practicing eating meditation. Feel the movement of your breath carrying aromas in the Air.

Notice your hand reaching for the fork. Feel the extension of the arm as the element of Earth.

If the food is warm or hot, notice the Fire element. If the food is cold, notice the absence of the Fire element.

While chewing, feel the Earth element of teeth grinding the Earth and Water elements of food. Notice the Water element of saliva. Notice change of texture in the food.

Do you breathe—the Air element—before you swallow, or afterwards?

THE FIVE HINDRANCES

I F ASKED TO LIST THE obstacles to our gardening, we might name conditions like weather, time, water, and physical limitations, such as a bad back. Inner blocks might include impatience, lack of energy, and not really knowing what we should be doing in our garden.

The impediments in our path are called the Hindrances. The Buddha identified five such Hindrances.

Sense Desire
Ill Will
Sloth and Torpor
Restlessness and Anxiety
Skeptical Doubt

Recognizing these hurdles requires some effort. Although all of us experience all the Hindrances, there may be two or three with which we are best acquainted.

In the spring I sometimes come home from a nursery or garden center with a trunk full of plants (Sense Desire), which then languish beside the front step because I don't know where to plant them (Doubt). Every time I walk in or out of the house I look at them and wonder when I'm going to get around to planting (Ill Will toward myself). Eventually I walk around the garden, plant in one hand, shovel in the other. "Here?" I wonder. "No. Maybe over there" (Restlessness and Anxiety). Sometimes I forget about these plants in pots until October (Sloth), when I finally notice them again and just plop them into my holding bed.

During meditation, the Hindrances prevent Concentration from arising. In our daily lives, they block beneficial states of Mind, such as Loving-Kindness, Joy, and the rest of the Perfections (*Paramis*).

Sense Desire

In January, I sit down one evening with a stack of seed and plant catalogs and a yellow highlighter. As I turn the pages, I mark the seeds or plants I want and then dog-ear the pages. Each seed packet costs only $2.25 and I keep thinking, "Oh, yes. That one. And this pink poppy looks so pretty. Ooh. Nasturtiums." The next evening I fill out the order forms, and the total is almost a hundred dollars.

Some years ago I developed a passion for astilbes.... So now I wanted all the astilbes in the catalogues—short and tall, early, midsummer, and late, white, peach-colored, rose and those copper-foliaged red ones that glow like torches and would light up the dark places under the trees.

Elisabeth Sheldon

Sense Desire belongs to the Greed family and includes mental desires, as well as a gardener's desire—for color, texture, and fragrance.

Carol Young, a gardening friend, says that when she goes plant shopping she goes crazy. We desire something, we buy it, we're satisfied for a little while; and then the wanting starts again. We think that buying more plants will assuage our desire, but desire always returns.

What actually satisfies desire is not obtaining the next new plant but stopping desire itself. This may sound like a koan.[26] How can you stop desire without satisfying it?

Being in debt to desire is like being in credit card debt—you continually have to work to pay off what you owe. You fulfill one hankering and another arises: desire begins again, and you want something more. The credit card bill just keeps escalating.

Sense Desire Investigation

What do your senses desire? Which of these are the most important, or least important, to you?

Most Important	*Least Important*	
		sounds
		colors
		forms and shapes
		textures
		body sensations (inner)
		tactile sensations (outer)
		smells
		tastes
		thoughts

THE MEDITATIVE GARDENER

Ill Will

A gardening friend, walking through my garden, spotted a clump of green bishop's weed (*Aegopodium*). "Oh, look," she said. "You've got Enemy."

At that time I was not yet acquainted with the invasive nature of bishop's weed and how it grows from the tiniest rootlet left in the ground.

What are the particular weeds or so-called flowers that you think of as your enemies? Dandelions, bindweed, or crabgrass might inspire this feeling of Ill Will. What's your personal nemesis?

Ill Will belongs to the family of Aversion and is familiar to us as the judging, comparing Mind that we experience when we hear garden snobbery. "Oh, begonias! They are so common. I mean, really, you'd think people could be more creative. " Yes. Class distinction happens even in a garden.

Loving Your Enemy Contemplation

Once in a while you can convert to loving your enemy with a simple paradigm shift. For instance, I overheard one gardener say to another, "You don't like bats? I like bats. Anything that eats mosquitoes is a friend of mine."

> A weed is no more than a flower in disguise.
>
> James Russell Lowell

In the early 1980s, the first spring that Laotian and Cambodian refugees were living in our community, they saw dandelions and thought them beautiful. When I looked at dandelions as if for the first time I began to see how bright and cheery they are. When I was growing up we would go out to the lawn with a paring knife in the early, early spring to dig young dandelion greens. My father loved wilted-dandelion-green salad.

A friend took her grandson to a retreat center with a prayer wheel. Now her grandchild delights in dandelion seed puffs, calling them flower prayer wheels.

List some weeds that you don't like—not the ones you hate, but the weeds that irritate you.

Are any of these plants edible (even if you yourself might not eat them)? Medicinal? Decorative? Do they attract wildlife?

Are there any weeds or critters you can actually sort of appreciate because of a benefit they provide?

Getting to Know Your Enemy Contemplation

> What is a weed? A plant whose virtues have not yet been discovered.
>
> Ralph Waldo Emerson

Getting to know your enemy can provide a slow shift away from pure Ill Will. Reading a weed book,[27] I learned that plantain indicates compacted dirt. No wonder it grows in the driveway! Dandelions and other tap-rooted weeds bring up needed minerals from deep in the soil. I still pull dandelions, but I often lay them to rest in a flower bed where their mineral-rich roots decompose into the top layer of soil. Sheep sorrel suggests acid soil—the bigger the leaves, the more acidic. Pineapple weed denotes crusty soil. Goldenrods, asters, and wild lettuce grow in sandy soil. Thistles are rich in potassium. Chickweed and creeping speedwell denote substantial shade. Clovers, vetch, and birdsfoot trefoil indicate low nitrogen. Dock, mullein, hawkweed, sheep sorrel, and wild strawberry reveal low pH. Mullein, wild carrot, wild parsnip, wild radish, foxtail grass, and mallow indicate low fertility. Spurge, crabgrass, pigweed, yarrow, yellow wood sorrel, and curly dock grow in dry soil.

Often weeds are communicating something to us about the soil. What's the message your weeds are sending you?

Weeding Meditation #2

How can you put Ill Will to rest for awhile without cultivating Aversion to it? The surprising and simple answer is Mindfulness. An unwholesome state of Mind such as Aversion cannot co-exist with a wholesome state of Mind such as Mindfulness. So we don't have to do anything about Ill Will or try to respond differently. Simply being mindful is sufficient.

I appreciate the misunderstanding I have had with Nature over my perennial border. I think it is a flower garden; she thinks it is a meadow lacking grass and tries to correct the error.

Sara Stein

As you pull up an enemy weed, note, "Ill Will. Ill Will."

Search to feel whether or not this is true for you.

Notice little shreds of Ill Will such as "I don't like you" or "I don't want you growing here" or "You bother me."

Can you lovingly pull a weed?

Practice this meditation for the entire time you are weeding today.

Sloth and Torpor

Armchair gardeners may recognize this particular Hindrance. People who love gardens but who do not love to garden may find it difficult to overcome inertia. "I'm too tired," they say. Or, "I'll get around to it later."

The sloth is a graceful, deliberate creature that hangs from tropical treetops, has an extremely slow metabolism, and sleeps fifteen hours a day.

While Sloth or lethargy denotes a heaviness of Body, Torpor or drowsiness refers to a dullness of Mind. The torporous Mind slides off the meditation object—such as the breath or a Contemplation—as if it's slipping on a patch of ice. Once it's in the prone position, so to speak, the Mind decides it is much easier to stay there than to find firm ground. When I cannot remember a meditation instruction five seconds after it is given, I know that Torpor is enticing me with forgetfulness. I have spent many retreats investigating Torpor, one breath at a time, which at least keeps me alert to its seductive sleepiness.

You can recognize Torpor during the early days of a meditation retreat by those who are dozing on the cushion and practicing "head bobbing meditation."

Sloth and Torpor are like a stagnant pond; Energy is stuck. The traditional remedy is to live in open air, change posture, and change light. It sounds as if gardening itself is the cure. If Sloth or Torpor bothers you, arouse Energy to take yourself out to the garden or to stand up during your meditation session.

Energy Investigation #1

A hyperactive friend says she has two speeds: "High" and "Off."

What do you have Energy for?

When does Energy leave you stranded?

THE MEDITATIVE GARDENER

Restlessness and Anxiety

Our culture excels in the worry-flurry of too many things to do, too many places to go, too many garden catalogs to read, and not enough time to do it all. Multi-tasking seems to be the answer, but, in fact, the Mind can only fully attend to one thing at a time. Those things in our peripheral awareness are not receiving our complete attention. Besides, the list of tasks is endless.

The garden is a place to which we go for relief from the intensity of daily life, yet even here we may rush to get a job done or obsess about how it looks and whether we've done it right.

I am one of those people who have at least four projects going at the same time. On the one hand, varying physical positions prevents me from over-stressing muscles and joints. But I move from weeding to transplanting to hauling to dead-heading mostly because I have a short attention span. I get tired of weeding, and allow my Body to go wherever my Mind wants it to go. I leave the bucket by the spot where I've been weeding, because I think I'll be right back. Then when I'm cooking supper, I look out the window and there's the bucket, a shovel, the garden cart, or a trowel at the edge of a flower bed. If it's started to sprinkle, my sweetie says, "Don't you think you should bring your tools in out of the rain?"

As you have doubtless discovered in meditation, the Body wants to move when the Mind is moving. "Doing" masks dukkha (Stress).

Restlessness is like a strong wind blowing over a pond because we haven't found what we want. Some desire is arising though the desire cannot be satisfied. Wishes also create Restlessness; I wish a particular flower bed looked better than it does, so I embark on weeding, transplanting, pruning, but something else catches my attention and I move on.

While Restlessness denotes an excess of Energy in the Body, Anxiety results from an excess of Energy in the Mind.

My local gardening group tours my garden in the early spring when the daffodils are blooming. I have a good selection of bulbs and a nice collection of early spring bloomers, including ephemeral wildflowers. The blast of color in the flower beds while the tree leaves are still lettuce green gives us all cause for Joy.

Some years the snow banks don't melt until a couple of weeks before the tour, so I have to rush to mulch all the beds, edge some of them, and clip and clean. Beech leaves that have clung to their branches all winter don't fall until just a few days before the tour, so I have to rake the lawn—again—or race around with the lawnmower to chop the tan papery leaves to bits.

My Mind begins to worry, "Will I get it all done? What will they think if they see weeds in the flower beds?" I want the gardens to look nice for visitors, but can I do it?

Wanting to know the unknowable future gives rise to Anxiety, because that Sense Desire (of the Mind) can never ever be satisfied. The Energy of springtime and doing and the worrying Mind outweighs the steadiness of the Body, and perhaps its ability too.

Restlessness and Anxiety Investigation

What causes you to become anxious or worried in your daily life?

Are you anxious about anything in the garden?

Are you anxious about anything regarding your meditation?

When do you become restless?

Are you restless while you are in the garden?

Do you become restless while you are meditating? Is there a thought that causes that Restlessness to arise?

Skeptical Doubt

My neighbor Lynn Levine[28] asked several women friends to a weekend in a drafty log cabin (with a great woodstove!) in a forest preserve to celebrate her birthday. When we woke up the first morning, the woods were covered with three inches of snow! It was May! Undeterred, we set out across an open field on a planned wild-flower walk. Midway across the field a line of tracks crossed our path. A fox! The

tracks went from west to east, then turned back west, then zigzagged east again. The fox had set out on a purpose. Then something happened to make it change its Mind, and it turned around. Then it changed its Mind again and returned to its original course and continued across the field. That zigzag of tracks in the snow is a perfect picture of Doubt.

You have an intention. Something happens. You change your Mind. This change of Mind stops you in your tracks.

How often on my way to the vegetable garden, do I suddenly stop and think, "Hey. As long as I'm going to pick a tomato, why don't I take out the clippers and cut some flowers as well?" I backtrack, zigzag and eventually continue on my course.

The same thing happens in our meditation practice. "Yes. I'm going to do that gardening meditation," you think. Then something happens. The Mind wanders away to something else. "Well, is that gardening meditation really so important after all?" it asks.

Buddhist texts compare Skeptical Doubt to being on a perilous journey through the desert. Do you really trust the directions to the oasis? To stay the course requires resolution; the only other option is to wander for miles in the sand and risk dying of thirst.

Skeptical Doubt is counteracted by faith. Do you trust this path? Do you trust the teacher? Do you trust the instructions?

You don't need much faith—just enough to take you out to the garden today or enough to sit to the end of your meditation. Just enough to follow through on your decision to garden with a meditative Mind.

Investigating Skeptical Doubt

Do you have any doubts about your gardening abilities? About your gardening?

Are you skeptical about your meditation practice? Your teacher? This book?

Summary

Among the Five Hindrances we meet the Three Roots of Stress:

Sense Desire, which is a form of Greed
Ill Will, which is a form of Aversion
Skeptical Doubt, which is a form of Delusion

Sloth and Torpor can arise when there's a subtle Ill Will toward the meditation object that manifests as boredom followed by oh-so-pleasant drowsiness or lethargy, which is a form of Sense Desire.

Restlessness and Anxiety increase when a Sense Desire cannot be satisfied, thereby creating Ill Will toward the present moment.

Most likely we come to meditation in the first place to find a place of Calm or maybe a quiet happiness, yet the Mind wanders off in all directions. By categorizing these wanderings into the Five Hindrances, we are applying Mindfulness. As we bring Mindfulness to the Hindrances, we become aware of their arising and ceasing.

When the Hindrances are temporarily held at bay, Concentration increases.

It's like weeds: when we do nothing in the garden the weeds smother all the beautiful plants. Weeds rob the other plants of nourishment, or rain and sun, and if we can't eradicate them because their roots are too deep and powerful, we can at least cut them back so that they get smaller and weaker. And that's exactly what happens through the meditative absorptions. We don't uproot the hindrances, but we make them smaller.

Ayya Khema

Hindrances Inquiry

Which of the Hindrances hinder your Concentration?

_____   *Sense Desire*

_____   *Ill Will*

_____   *Sloth and Torpor*

_____   *Restlessness/Anxiety/worry and flurry*

_____   *Skeptical Doubt*

Can you rank the Hindrances from most hindering to least?

THE SEVEN FACTORS
FOR AWAKENING

GARDEN DESIGNERS TELL US TO choose three or five or seven species of plants and use them repeatedly throughout our gardens in order to achieve a consistency of appearance. The Seven Factors for Awakening are the qualities we want to consistently propagate in our inner gardens.

The Factors for Awakening form a habitat. When one grows, the others will also naturally arise, one after the other. The Seven Factors are:

Mindfulness
Investigation
Energy
Joy
Calm
Concentration
Equanimity

In the spring I look carefully (Mindfulness) at the seedlings growing in my flower beds. I determine which are weeds and which are annuals, biennials, or perennials that I actually want (Investigation). As I look at the long flower bed stretching out before me, I feel enthusiastic (Energy) about being outdoors in the garden. When I find tiny columbines, poppies, or larkspurs growing, I feel very happy (Joy). At some point during my gardening day, a feeling of Calm or peace may arise. Then I lose track of time (Concentration) and realize there's no place else I'd rather be. When I find a dead chipmunk, chin resting on paws, lying under the big, shady leaves of a violet, I think if I died right now I would feel content (Equanimity).

My gardening mentor, Ruth Marx, tells me to have one "showstopper" plant in each garden bed each season, one that grabs everyone's attention.

The Seven Factors for Awakening have the capacity to stop the show. The "show" is Delusion itself. Waking up implies that we have been in a dream state. This dreamy state—we are so familiar with it that we call it "reality"—is Delusion.

According to Dipa Ma,[29] an Asian teacher who has inspired many Westerners, the purpose of a human life is to experience the first stage of Awakening. (There are four such stages.)[30] The first stage, called stream entry, can occur only when all Seven Factors for Awakening are present.

> Row, row, row your boat,
> gently down the stream.
> Merrily, merrily, merrily, merrily.
> Life is but a dream.

Some meditators subscribe to the idea of sudden awakening. It is true that a beautiful Mind state may suddenly and unexpectedly flower just as an extraordinary specimen may sudden bloom in the woods or the prairie or the desert.

Yet this meditation practice focuses on what is referred to as a gradual awakening. The light of Wisdom dawns slowly, as we gradually retrain our Minds, turning them away from unwholesome qualities and towards the Factors for Awakening. As a gardener I appreciate cultivating an environment where wholesome seeds and wholesome roots can grow and bloom and where weeds slowly but surely diminish and can even be entirely uprooted.

After 20 years of gardening I discovered a lady's slipper blooming in the woods beside my driveway. However, after flowering for three springs, it stopped, because the area had become too shady. The conditions for its continued flowering were not being met. Similarly, a sudden opening of awareness often shifts as our inner and outer environmental circumstances change.

Mindfulness

The very first quality that we are encouraged to cultivate on this path is Mindfulness. We plant, water, and nourish the seed of Mindfulness by sitting each day and by carrying Mindfulness with us as we go about our daily life, including gardening.

As I mentioned earlier, for my first many years practicing meditation, I would meditate for a few months, then stop for a couple of months, then go on a retreat, then not go on a retreat for a few years. As you can guess, this does not much Mindfulness produce! Imagine if you treated your garden this erratically!

Mindfulness is the beginning, middle, and end of our path. It is so important that it appears in many of the Buddhist "lists" we have talked about. We begin learning to meditate by becoming mindful of the breath. Already we have encountered the Four Foundations of Mindfulness—Body, Feelings, Mind, and Contemplations. Now we meet Mindfulness as a Factor that can wake us up.

Once we begin watering the seed of Mindfulness regularly, we practice Wise Mindfulness, one step of the Buddhist eightfold path. Mindfulness is also one of the five faculties to help overcome the Hindrances.

The Mind has a unique ability to reflect upon itself. Our other senses simply do their jobs—the eyes see, the ears hear, the tongue tastes, the nose smells, and the Body feels. The Mind not only thinks, it is also aware that it is thinking. (And it can also be aware that it is aware of thinking!) We use this ability of the Mind to reflect upon itself—Mindfulness—as our springboard to waking up. Thus, Mindfulness is always useful in every situation. We can't have too much Mindfulness.

The Dharma is like a hologram: each piece of the Dharma projects the entire image, the entire teachings, but from a different view. Every time we meet Mindfulness on our path, and by now we have encountered it repeatedly, we see it from a slightly different angle.

The mind without mindfulness is sometimes compared to a pumpkin, the mind established in mindfulness to a stone. A pumpkin placed on the surface of a pond soon floats away and always remains on the water's surface. But a stone does not float away; it stays where it is put and at once sinks into the water until it reaches bottom. Similarly, when mindfulness is strong, the mind stays with its object and penetrates its characteristics deeply. It does not wander and merely skim the surface as the mind destitute of mindfulness does.

Bhikkhu Bodhi

Opening the Field of Awareness Meditation

Now that we've focused on one sense at a time, one Feeling at a time, one Mind state at a time, let's allow our attention to open wide, like the panoramic lens of a camera. This practice of open attention can help us to bring Mindfulness more fully into every moment of our lives.

When you are in the garden today, allow awareness to move to whichever Foundation of Mindfulness predominates at the moment— Body, Feelings, or Mind.

Be mindful of the Body and its many positions and sensations. Allow awareness to move to whatever sense door opens—hearing, touching, seeing, or smelling.

Be mindful of Feelings–pleasant, unpleasant, or neutral.

Be mindful of the moment when you notice that the Mind has wandered away. Label the thought "past" or "future" and return to present-moment Mindfulness of the Body, Feelings, and Mind, allowing the attention to rest on whatever aspect predominates.

Investigation

When something goes right or wrong in the garden, we investigate the causes and conditions that led to beautiful broccoli, perfect peppers, or lovely lilies. Was it this year's weather, soil amendments, or the variety we planted? What did we do differently? Or the same?

Because I am a Master Gardener, people frequently ask me questions about sick or failing plants or what to do about pests or where to plant their new perennial. They are trying to figure out how to become better gardeners themselves.

Investigation aids our meditation practice too. When a beautiful Mind state arises, look at it. Ask questions. How did it come about? What was happening just before it arose? What are the qualities of this Mind state? How was the quality maintained? Did something contribute to its passing? Also, ask questions of your teachers.

The Buddha encouraged us not to take his word for it, but to investigate for ourselves whether his teachings are true. If you've read this far, you've already begun to investigate the truth of this path for yourself.

Investigation Contemplation

Think of one of your own recent beautiful Mind states embodying Calm, happiness, Joy, peace, tranquility, or sweetness—something that makes you smile.

Recall to the best of your ability the experience of that beneficial Mind state. Feel it in your Body. Where in the Body does that feeling reside?

How did the wholesome Mind state arise? What were you thinking or doing just before it happened?

How did you maintain that state?

How did that beautiful Mind state end? What did you do or think that caused it to dissipate?

The rational Mind may not be able to answer all or any of these questions today. Allow the asking to be enough. Trust your intuition to eventually discover an answer. An insight will come.

Energy

The sun shines on our gardens and provides Energy for plants to grow. The seedlings in my solarium get leggy and fall over if they don't get enough sun in the early spring. Likewise, our meditation practice collapses into drowsiness and lethargy if we don't bring enough Energy to bear. The Hindrance of Sloth and Torpor can be counteracted by finding a source of Energy.

What energizes your meditation—or your gardening?

Since sitting still with my eyes closed can make my Body think it's time for a nap, I first spend a few moments expressing gratitude and Loving-Kindness for the things I love about my life. This practice makes me smile; the Mind brightens and becomes happy and that happiness fuels my meditation.

Too much Energy results in the Hindrance of Restlessness and Anxiety. The restless Body wants to move, and the anxious Mind to obsess. A surplus of Energy can be counterbalanced by Concentration, another Factor for Awakening.

Energy Investigation #2

Examine your biorhythms:

When during the day does the high point of your Energy occur? When is your low point?

What time(s) of day do you like to garden?

What time(s) of day do you like to meditate?

What time is too early for you to meditate? What time is too late? What time is too sluggish?

Joy

Our gardens must bring us some form of happiness; otherwise we would not continue getting ourselves hot, dirty, sweaty, and bitten by bugs for the sake of a few flowers or vegetables. As gardeners, we continue to exert Energy on a regular basis, and that Energy brings us the Joy of being in the garden, the Joy of seeing flowers bloom, cutting flowers for a bouquet, harvesting and eating our very own vegetables.

Where do we find Joy in our meditation practice? We need to en-joy some aspect of meditating; otherwise we will never sit down long enough to practice. So much en-joy-ment can be found in the world, some of my friends cannot figure out why I bother meditating. My Joy bubbles up in the solitude of the early morning hours and gives rise to a quiet happiness. This is a natural time to meditate before my Mind revs up to meet the day. Once I'm on the cushion, I love doing the Contemplations in this book and investigating the Mind. After visiting my gardens, I look forward to meditating with my neighbors at 8:00 A.M. because we learn so much from each other.

Thich Nhat Hanh advises us to wear a half-smile during meditation. In doing this, he suggests, we are nurturing peace and Joy. If putting on a smile feels false to you, then try this: Notice the corners of your mouth when you are in the garden today. Do you feel them turning down in a scowl? Do the muscles relax a bit when you're more at ease? What about when you're happy?

The very act of planting a seed in the earth has in it to me something beautiful. I always do it with a joy that is largely mixed with awe.

Celia Thaxter

Harvesting Meditation

As you pick vegetables from your garden, note how you feel. Excited? Happy? Thankful? Joyful? Do you have a smile on your face as you bend over, stretch out your hand, and pull?

Don't let yourself be distracted by thinking about something else. Don't focus on irritation with pests or on what you have to do five minutes from now. Concentrate on the emotion you feel when you are harvesting and continue to attend to the feeling as you fill your harvest basket and carry your vegetables into the house.

When you cook the vegetables, note again how you feel about making something to eat that you grew in your very own garden.

Continue to focus on your particular variety of happiness.

Can you locate it in your Body?

Gratitude Meditation

In August and September one of my favorite things is to make a salsa, which I call "Garden in a Bowl." I dice up an onion and a pepper and add ¼ cup umeboshi plum vinegar. I cut up a cucumber or use the tomatillos that ripen later in the season. I chop up several tomatoes—cherry tomatoes early in the season—smoosh a few cloves of garlic, and sliver cilantro leaves. Ahh! Everything directly from the garden. Everything directly from *my* garden.

When I sit down to a bowl of the salsa I feel so happy and grateful to the garden. Often I say a few words of thanks to the vegetables themselves, the plants, the sun, and the rain, the farmer who sold me the pepper plants, and anyone and anything else I can think of.

Remember to say a few words of thanks before dining on your garden feast.

Over time gratitude for all things large and small feeds the feeling of Joy.

A Bouquet of Joy

As you pick some flowers from your garden, notice how you feel. Pay attention to your emotions as you see a flower, consider it, and cut it to add to the collection already in your hand.

Look at your bouquet-in-progress. How do you feel? Don't be distracted by thoughts of bouquet incompetence. Notice the feeling of happiness or pleasure, even though it may be very small. What would you call that emotion? Where does it reside in your Body?

After you've arranged your bouquet, stand back and admire it. Continue to focus on happiness, satisfaction, or well-being and feel how it feels. Close your eyes if that helps.

Disregard for the moment the pull to go on to the next thing.

Consider giving your bouquet away. (Note any thoughts of "mine" or "It's so pretty. I think I'll keep it.")

If you do give it away, notice whether the giving increased your pleasure.

Calm

One reason many gardeners give for gardening is that it gives them a sense of peace. Calm or tranquility or serenity follows naturally on the heels of Joy. Fully satisfied, the Mind comes to rest, not wishing for anything else at the moment.

> Breathing in, I calm Body and Mind.
> Breathing out, I smile.
>
> Thich Nhat Hanh

On one long retreat, I did the first sitting of the afternoon beside a pond. Basking in the sun and listening to the sounds of water creatures made me very happy—joyful, you could say. Then I did walking meditation beside the retreat center's vegetable garden, which I enjoyed tremendously because I was missing my own vegetable garden. I went into the meditation hall for the next sit and spent much of it noticing little shards of Hindrances as they arose. Then, as often happens, just before the bell rang signaling the end of the sit, a wide space of Calm opened up.

Calming Contemplation

Sit comfortably, feeling the Body rooted to the earth.

   Then notice the place of still water within.

   Notice where in the Body this place of stillness is located. Become familiar with it over time.

   Notice this Calm feeling when it arises. Make space for it.

   Where in your Body does Calm abide?

Dwell as near as possible to the channel in which your life flows.

Henry David Thoreau

Concentration

Phyllis Young, another gardening friend, says that time stops for her when she's in the garden.

Imagine being as absorbed in meditation as you can be in the garden. This factor of absorption is called Concentration. Concentration means being entirely engrossed in what you are doing. Athletes call this sort of Concentration "the Zone." Artists call this one-pointedness of Mind "Flow."

During meditation, Concentration in the form of meditative absorption arises only when the five Hindrances are kept in abeyance, even temporarily, through the simple act of Mindfulness.

If your Mind doesn't stay in one place, it's like standing on a lawn: If you stand in ten different places, the grass will grow in all ten places, because first you stand here for a while and then go stand there for a while and then go stand over there. If you don't stay long in any one place, grass will grow everywhere. But if you really stand still in one place, how will the grass grow there? No grass will be able to grow on the spot where the soles of your feet are standing. In the same way, if your Mind stands firm in one place, always Mindful of the in-and-out breath, no Hindrances or defilements will be able to arise.

Ajaan Lee Dhammadaro

Concentration Investigation

Do you ever lose track of time when you're in the garden?

How about when you are meditating?

What activities are most likely to lead you into Concentration?

What are your indicators of "Flow" or being "in the Zone"?

Equanimity

"The Great Way is not difficult for those who have no preferences." Equanimity represents the balance of neither grasping for the pleasant nor pushing away the unpleasant. This seeing "things as they are" allows the Mind to rest deeply in a place of stillness, a place of non-reaction.

Sometimes my beloved and I discuss what our future might be after the other one dies. Since he definitely does not garden, he sometimes half-teases me by saying he's going to plant my hillside gardens in pachysandra or myrtle (*Vinca*) so he can just mow the lawn (which he does enjoy) and have a nice-looking yard without the gardening. So I go about my weeding and transplanting and dead-heading with the full knowledge that this garden I love is subject to all sorts of changes. Once in a while I sit on the deck and imagine I am looking at nothing but lawn and pachysandra. For a moment I let go of my preference for flower beds and my ideas of what is aesthetically pleasing. For a moment I consider what would be easiest for his aging Body. For a moment I can see the flow of life.

The universe is a continuous web.
Touch it at any point and the whole web quivers.

Stanley Kunitz

Redwood Tree Contemplation

Imagine you are a redwood tree at least a thousand years old. Breathe in, breathe out. Feel yourself rooted to the earth.

From the vantage point of your height, look out at the world around you. You may notice that you are in a grove of redwood sisters. Perhaps your redwood children stand around you.

Think back on all the life you have seen over the past one or two thousand years. Remember all the lives you have watched come and go. Think of the arguments and wars you have observed come and go. Recall the tragedies of hundreds of years ago, past now and even forgotten.

How many times have you seen fire destroy life around you? Perhaps you yourself bear the scars of fire or even direct strikes by lightning. Yet those wounds healed, centuries ago.

Look out on the life around you. Feel the Equanimity of the long view.

Recollect any current problems or issues in your life, and look down on them from your great height and age.

Summary

The Buddha was sitting under a bodhi tree (*Ficus religiosa*) when he became enlightened. The Factors for Awakening are like seven branches of a tree, each limb supporting us to reach the next limb.

The more you cultivate the four foundations of Mindfulness, the more these factors of Enlightenment can be expected to grow.

Sangharakshita

·   ·   ·

Dedicating Your Work

As you go out to your garden today, say,
"I dedicate this garden to the Awakening of all beings."

THE DIVINE ABODES

IMAGINE WHAT YOUR INNER LANDSCAPE would look like if you took the time to cultivate the four wholesome emotions of Loving-Kindness, Compassion, Appreciative Joy, and Equanimity. Picture yourself abiding in the garden of Loving-Kindness, resting in a bed of Compassion, standing in an arbor of Appreciative Joy, and gazing into a still lake of Equanimity. These qualities create excellent conditions for spiritual growth. Because of this, they are called the Divine Abodes.

People of all spiritual and religious persuasions aspire to live a life closer to the Divine. The Divine within us knows that just as we want to be happy, so every other person wants to be happy. A version of the Golden Rule—"Do unto others as you would have others do unto you."—can be found in every religion.[31]

Yet this "rule," which I learned as a child, was soon lost in the throes of my growing ego. The "I" wants to come first.

Each of the Divine Abodes, which are also called Heavenly Houses or the Four Immeasurables, has a Near Enemy and a Far Enemy. The Far Enemy is the obvious opposite of the Divine Abode. The Near Enemy is an emotion that looks very similar to the Divine Abode but is tinged with the self-interest of "Me first."

As a child, it took me years to distinguish between ragweed and tomato plants. They looked so much alike that I had to stop and puzzle over every ragweed I saw. Why would a tomato plant be growing in the driveway? Recognizing the characteristics that distinguish one look-alike plant from another required discernment; one needs to bring similar perspicacity to the task of distinguishing a Divine Abode from its Near Enemy.

The Divine is looking for a win-win situation as one practices love toward oneself and toward another person. The Near Enemy wants me and mine to win before the

other person wins. The Far Enemy wants the other person to lose without realizing that the "me" also loses because the resulting emotions—of hatred or anger, cruelty, envy, or Anxiety—all induce some form of personal Suffering.

Loving-Kindness (*Metta or Maitri*)

In ancient Greek five words were used for love:

> *eros* – sexual or physical love
> *storge* – family or natural affection
> *phileo*[32] – friendly affection
> *xenia*[33] – hospitality, the friendship between host and guest
> *agape* – Godlike or Divine love

One of the great satisfactions of the human spirit is to feel that one's family extends across the borders of the species and belongs to everything that lives. I feel I'm not only sharing the planet, but also sharing my life, as one does with a domestic animal. Certainly this is one of the great joys of living in this garden.

Stanley Kunitz

Paul Farmer, a doctor with Partners in Health who has dedicated his life to working with world's poorest people in Haiti[34] and elsewhere, displays on his laptop's home page two photographs side by side—one of his own child and one of a Haitian child. How many of us would present the photo of an anonymous child, or even of a neighbor's child? Would we place such photos beside those of our own children on our desks at work or on our bookshelves at home?

Imagine how you feel when someone hurts your nearest and dearest. From the Near Enemy of attachment, it's only a short step to Aversion, one of the Roots of Stress and the Far Enemy of Loving-Kindness.

The word "Kindness" comes from the same root as "kin" and "kindred." It may be easy to treat our kin and our kindred spirits with Kindness, but we also know that clannishness gives rise to many of the world's trouble spots. Extending our definition of kin also extends our feelings of Kindness.

Loving-Kindness is most similar to agape, a love showered on all beings equally and impartially.

Sowing in the morning, sowing seeds of kindness,
Sowing in the noontide and the dewy eve;
Waiting for the harvest, and the time of reaping,
We shall come rejoicing, bringing in the sheaves.

Knowles Shaw

The bumper sticker "Practice random kindness and senseless acts of beauty" speaks to the impartial nature of Loving-Kindness.

And then there's the bumper sticker that says, "Practice random acts of gardening."

Agapanthus comes from the Greek words "agape" and "anthos" meaning flower of love.

Ecumenical Loving–Kindness Meditation

Imagine you are being held in the hands of The Master Gardener. Sit or walk in your garden and say these phrases of Loving-Kindness to yourself: "May I feel safe. May I feel happy. May I feel strong. May I feel peaceful."

Offer your Loving-Kindness phrases to a mentor or person who has supported you in your life. "May you feel safe. May you feel happy. May you feel strong. May you feel peaceful."

To your nearest and dearest. "May you feel safe. May you feel happy. May you feel strong. May you feel peaceful."

To your good friends. "May you feel safe. May you feel happy. May you feel strong. May you feel peaceful."

To a neutral person, whose name you may not even know "May you feel safe. May you feel happy. May you feel strong. May you feel peaceful."

To someone you hold a slight grudge against. "May you feel safe. May you feel happy. May you feel strong. May you feel peaceful."

From your vantage point in the hands of The Master Gardener, look out over your community and say your phrases of Loving-Kindness. "May you feel safe. May you feel happy. May you feel strong. May you feel peaceful."

As you remain in the hands of The Master Gardener, say, "May all beings feel safe. May all beings feel happy. May all beings feel strong. May all beings feel peaceful."

Compassion (*Karuna*)[35]

Compassion is the heart that feels the Suffering of the world, and in today's world that needs to be a very big heart indeed. The phrases for Compassion are, "May your pain and Suffering come to an end. May you find peace."

In Hebrew, compassion has the same root as the word womb, which helps us understand the deep concern embodied in this quality of caring. In the Mahayana Buddhist tradition, the female Bodhisattva,[36] Kuan Yin, represents Compassion.

When I visited a Kuan Yin temple in Honolulu, just outside the gates of Foster Botanical Garden, I simply sat and looked at the statue of Kuan Yin. What I saw was a menopausal, slightly overweight woman with jowls–a woman who had seen a lot of life, a woman who knew everything. Apples, oranges, and other offerings were piled on the altar in front of her. A recent Southeast Asian immigrant came up to me and said, "Kuan Yin is the same as the Virgin Mary and Avalokitesvara,"[37] By this he meant that all three represent the spirit of Compassion. It is sometimes said that the Dalai Lama is an embodiment of Avalokitesvara, a Buddha incarnate.

While Loving-Kindness is the heart's natural response to another being, Compassion is the heart's response to seeing another living being suffer. This includes watching someone wrestle with her particular Root of Stress. After diagnosing myself as an aversive personality type, I now easily recognize others in my "family" of Aversion. I used to use defend myself from feeling their Suffering by thinking "That's not right… If they'd only…They should…." Nowadays, when I watch another aversive person struggle to halt what's unpleasant (by complaining, judging, or expressing annoyance) I recognize a pattern that is deeply familiar to me—and, rather than feeling repelled by that person's actions or speech, my heart opens to them.

When we feel Compassion, we, like Kuan Yin or the Dalai Lama, feel connected to other beings. If another person is in pain or is Suffering, we feel with and for them. We do not feel cut off. When we remove ourselves, we are not feeling Compassion, but rather its Near Enemy, pity. We think: "Oh. Those poor people." or "Those misguided souls." This sort of sympathy allows a corner of the heart to remain closed by the self-interest of "Well. At least it's not me," or "There but for the grace of God go I."

Compassion Meditation

The next time you are in the garden, think of someone who is having a difficult time right now.

Repeat to yourself, "May your pain and Suffering come to an end. May you find peace."

Invite the garden to support your Compassion.

THE MEDITATIVE GARDENER

Tonglen Meditation[38]

Tonglen is a Tibetan word that means giving and receiving.

Begin by doing *tonglen* for someone you care about and wish to help. Or, if you are stuck in a painful situation, do the practice for the pain you are feeling and simultaneously for all those like you who suffer the same feelings.

> *Sitting comfortably, rest your Mind briefly, for a second or two, in a state of openness or stillness.*
>
> *Breathe sorrows into your heart, dissolve them and breathe out a feeling of Compassion.*
>
> *Breathe in a feeling of hot, dark, and heavy, and breathe out a feeling of cool, bright, and light. Breathe in completely, through all the pores of your Body, and breathe out, radiate out, through all the pores of your Body.*
>
> *Include more than just that one person. Extend your meditation to others who are in the same situation. Breathe in their pain and send them relief.*

Contemplations ✧ *The Divine Abodes* 221

THE FAR ENEMY OF COMPASSION is cruelty, which we can easily imagine happening in war or in abusive situations.

War is commemorated in some park in every town and city in America and on at least three of our national holidays,[39] yet monuments to peace and peace gardens are few and far between. Peace gardens draw attention to the Suffering caused by war and arouse our Compassion for all concerned. Peace poles send the message "May peace prevail on earth" in different languages, one on each side of the four-, six- or eight-sided post.

> Old battlefield, fresh with spring flowers again.
> All that is left of the dreams
> of twice ten thousand warriors slain.
>
> Basho

Peace Pole Contemplation

Where in your garden or town would be an appropriate place for a peace pole?

let there be one hundred flowers
of peace that bloom in the garden

let there be one hundred hours
of peace for every moment of war

let there be one hundred acts
of kindness for each instance of hate

let there be one hundred years
of love for each minute of violence

let there be one hundred voices
of peace for each one of war

let there be one hundred flowers
of peace that bloom in the garden

T. Namaya

WHILE CRUELTY AND ABUSE ARE the obvious Far Enemies of Compassion, a less blatant and perhaps more familiar Far Enemy is the feeling of *Schadenfreude*—a German word meaning the delight in or enjoyment of another person's misfortune. For example, when Martha Stewart, the home and garden maven, went to jail for insider trading, who among us practiced Compassion for her? The far more likely response was a sort of gladness that she was being punished for breaking the rules.

Listening to the news is often a practice in Schadenfreude rather than Compassion. "The President (whoever he is) got what he deserved." Impending natural disasters can trigger a sort of thrill of anxiety. "What if the hurricane hits New Orleans?" I live in Red Sox-passionate New England. There is no love here for the New York Yankees, the Sox's longtime rivals. With the Sox-Yankee rivalry and others, all too often excitement over "our" win translates into happiness over the opponent's loss.

Then there are the events in our personal lives. When one friend tells of something bad happening to an acquaintance, and another gasps, "Oh, no!" have you ever looked down at the floor and smiled secretly?

Or consider those pesky bugs in your garden. Flicking them off of plants and into soapy water to drown is not pleasant. Yet, do you experience some relief at getting rid of them? I confess that I do. This relief is also a sort of Schadenfreude.

Schadenfreude Investigation

Today while you are in the garden, contemplate the following:
Can you think of any examples of cruelty, abuse, or Schadenfreude in your own life?

How might you practice Compassion in that situation, instead?

Are there particular bugs or pests that you exterminate from your garden? How do you feel about that?

How might you practice Compassion for the bugs?

Appreciative Joy *(Mudita)*

When my garden is in fullest bloom, I invite friends over for a tour of the flowers. One friend comes, stands at the corner of the house, puts her hands on her hips and glances at eight flower beds. "Great," she says, then turns around and leaves.

While visiting someone else's garden, how often does the comparing Mind leap to the fore? "My flower beds don't look that good," the Mind says, or "My gardens are better than this," as if gardening was a contest and there could be only one winner.

In our hearts we know that all gardeners "win" some Joy simply by being in the garden, no matter what the final product looks like. Can we feel happy for their Joy?

The Near Enemy of Appreciative Joy is the comparing Mind[40] and the insincere compliments or hypocritical comments that come to our lips as a result of a tiny (or big) inner competition we feel. Then, too, when someone tells us something good or fun or surprising about their lives, our customary response is to share our similar experience. Our intention is good, we want to connect with them by saying, "The same thing happened to me," but what happens is that we take the focus off the other person and train the spotlight on ourselves. We miss an opportunity to express directly to them, "How wonderful for you."

Sometimes we discount the other person by saying, "Oh, yeah. I've done that too," which has the effect of making their experience smaller.

Some people feel the inner competition so strongly that they immediately "one-up" you. "Nice daylilies. You should see mine. I have a purple daylily that is to die for."

My friend Lani Wright tells me about the subtle competition that happens on her block with three beautiful gardens. "You've been putting a lot of hours into the garden," one neighbor says to another. "Don't you think it's time to take a break?"

I'm an avid gardener, so visitors to my garden often say, "Boy. This is a lot of work."

All of a sudden, having a beautiful garden sounds *so* unpleasant, as if the Stress of gardening outweighs the pleasure of the beauty.

"This is my playground," I say, in an effort to shift the view to the pleasant scene in front of us.

Envy or covetousness is the Far Enemy of Appreciative Joy: we want what someone else has.

Think about your neighbor's garden, a good friend's garden, a gardening friend's garden. When you tour their gardens, how do you feel? Slightly covetous of particular plants or a design? Slightly condescending because your friend or neighbor doesn't understand some basic garden principles as well as you do?

It can be difficult to put to rest our opinions (about another's garden or even about our own gardening abilities) and simply feel happy for the good fortune that others are enjoying. Whether it's an elderly woman's single flower bed with one tomato plant that brings her so much Joy or the extensive gardens and paid gardeners of a well-to-do person, can we be happy simply for *their* happiness?

In English, there is no single word that expresses the opposite of envy. So we have to content ourselves with the phrase "Appreciative Joy"—being happy for the good fortune of others or Joy in their Joy. Appreciation has the double meaning of "recognizing with gratitude" and "increasing the value of." Just imagine "appreciating" your friend's garden—recognizing with gratitude the effort she puts into it and thereby increasing the personal value of her effort.

Redirecting the Mind to Appreciative Joy requires Wisdom, intention, and repeated effort. This happiness for others does not come easily. Appreciative Joy is said to be the most difficult Divine Abode to cultivate.

Appreciative Joy Meditation

Today while you are in the garden, visualize a friend's garden and the pleasure it brings her.

Now think of your friend and say, "May your good fortune continue."

Bring to Mind someone who has just had a stroke of luck or to whom something good has happened.

Say, "May your good fortune continue."

Think about people you know who have good relationships, beautiful homes, successful children, great jobs.

Whisper in your Mind, "May your good fortune continue."

Bring to Mind people who meditate regularly and go on retreat often or someone whom you think has spiritual attainments.

Say "May your good fortune continue."

Think of people who have what you want and wish them well: "May your good fortune continue."

Practice this meditation for as long as you are in the garden today.

Equanimity (*Upekka*)

The quality of Equanimity relies on a deep understanding of karma, which, in gardener's language, translates as, "You reap what you sow."

Realizing the truth of this proverb encourages us to be more mindful of the tiny seeds that we sow from moment to moment, which eventually turn into habits. We can never fully understand karma—the Buddha said that trying to understand the intricacies of karma will drive you crazy—but having some sense of the cycle of cause and effect turns out to be very helpful.

Perhaps no situation better tries our capacity for Equanimity than seeing our loved ones, especially our children, make unwise decisions. After spending years trying to help our children cultivate sound values and character, we can feel heartbroken watching them make choices we would not make.

The traditional phrases of Equanimity seem particularly appropriate in this situation. They are, "You are the owner of your actions, despite my best wishes for you."

·   ·   ·

Equanimity Meditation

Think of a recent upsetting event in your life in which you wanted another person to make a choice different from the one he or she actually made.

While keeping this person in Mind, repeat to yourself, "You are the owner of your actions, despite my best wishes for you."

Continue to contemplate this in the garden today.

THE NEAR ENEMY OF EQUANIMITY is indifference as expressed in a shrug of the shoulders and the expression, "whatever." Not caring is a way of protecting ourselves from our own emotions. The fatalism of "Well, that's just my karma this time around" may look like Equanimity, but it's actually the Near Enemy.

Fear underlies all the Near Enemies: attachment is the fear of separation, pity is the fear of feeling Suffering, envy is the fear of not having enough, and indifference is the fear of failure.

A friend took me on a walk through a few acres of her woodland. She had opened up the forest to expose rock walls, fern gardens, and a babbling brook. It was a lovely meditative walk. Then I noticed the understory of invasive bushes. "You sure have a lot of barberry growing here," I said. "Yes," she sighed. "You just can't do anything about it."

As a Plant Conservation Volunteer, I sometimes join teams of people working to control invasives. It is possible to diminish or even eradicate invasives, but it does require effort and Determination. Assuming that nothing can be done looks like equanimous acceptance. "That's just the way it is." But actually it's a fear of failure—"What if I do all that work, go to all that trouble, and nothing changes? After all, it's such a big problem. How could I possibly make a dent in it?"

The Far Enemy of Equanimity is Anxiety and Greed. As we know from our all-too-busy lives, multi-tasking breeds the Restlessness of "What next?" and the Anxiety of trying to "get it all done," while wondering whether what we're doing is good enough.

My own Restlessness takes the form of doing the next garden task I think of, which leads me from the herb garden to the shade garden to the vegetable garden at the other end of my property. I admire gardeners who can concentrate on one bed, one task at a time.

The greediness of desire can also lead to a restless scanning for the next pleasant thing. The mind that picks and chooses is still mired in grasping. An equanimous mind is content.

Summary

The Divine Abodes are the four divine emotions of Loving-Kindness, Compassion, Appreciative Joy, and Equanimity—attributes that we would expect any divine being to have. These qualities abide in our very selves. However, these heavenly states of Mind do require some cultivating, since we are much more familiar with the worldly emotions of mad, sad, glad, and scared.

A few years ago I had a falling-out with a friend. Every time my Mind revisited the unkind things she had said or the ways in which she didn't understand my point of view, I tried to turn my Mind to Loving-Kindness, instead. I could wish safety for her and good health. I could also wish peace for her (for then, I too would have peace). But I wasn't quite ready to wish her happiness. Continuing this practice of turning the Mind away from the unwholesome onto the wholesome for some months was one of the most difficult and most instructive experiences I have had as a meditator. I tried not to water the weeds of irritation, judgment, and self-defense, but instead turned the Mind slowly, slowly, bit by bit, toward Loving-Kindness, which I extended to her. It took months, but eventually I could wish her happiness. Months after that, I moved her out of the realm of "difficult person" and back to "friend."

The Divine Abodes shower Loving-Kindness, Compassion, Appreciative Joy, and Equanimity on all beings, impartially.

We should have love and compassion equally toward all people we meet. We can't just think, this one is not a friend or a relative, so therefore we don't need to have any concern for her. Actually we are all friends and relatives in birth. There are no other people. Even though we are from different townships or provinces, we are like grains of rice. They grow from one plant or in one field, and as they grow and increase, they are spread around and planted in other places. One grain makes a plant, one plant makes many grains that seed new plants. But it is still rice from the same plant spreading the species far and wide.

Ajahn Chah

THE THREE JEWELS

THE GARDEN IS OUR SANCTUARY, a place where we can find respite from the Stresses of the everyday world. As gardeners we are accustomed to going for refuge in our gardens.

So, too, as meditators in the Buddhist tradition, we regularly recite the going for refuge.

I go for refuge in the Buddha.
I go for refuge in the Dharma.
I go for refuge in the Sangha.

These phrases mean literally that we are going for refuge in Awakening (the Buddha being the Awakened One), in the teachings, and in our community of meditating friends. The Buddha, Dharma, and Sangha are the supports for our meditation practice. Without them, we could not proceed on this path.

When I tend the garden where my Buddha statue sits, I find that I naturally become more mindful of my work—transplanting vegetable seedlings, cultivating roses, weeding, or cutting flowers. No matter what I'm doing, I find I pay closer attention, as if the Buddha were watching me. Actually my own Buddha-nature *is* watching me. Then I remember: I am going for refuge in the possibility of my own Awakening.

One of my teachers James Baraz tells the story of Ram Dass asking him, "What do you love?" James replied, "The Dharma." I resonate with James' response and often draw upon my gratitude for these teachings as a way to summon Energy at the beginning of a meditation sitting.

The phrase "I go for refuge in the Dharma" takes on meaning as I discover the depth of the teachings and seek to apply them in my daily life. I am indeed deeply grateful for the Dharma.

I've been sitting with my sangha six mornings a week for many years now. This one hour at the beginning of the day is truly the place in which I go for refuge.

The refuges of Buddha, Dharma, and Sangha are not only sanctuaries of Calm, peace, serenity, and Joy. They are way stations on the road toward the ending of Stress and Suffering, a road that leads to our Awakening.

Meditation on the Three Refuges

At the beginning of your sitting meditation, say to yourself, "I go for refuge in the Buddha."

How does that statement feel? True? Foreign? Uncertain?

Then say, "I go for refuge in the Dharma."

How does that feel? Accurate? Relieving? Confusing?

And finally say, "I go for refuge in the Sangha" as you think of your meditating friends. If you don't have friends who meditate, think of the authors of Dharma books you have read.

How do you feel about this phrase? Deeply grateful? Cool? Unsure?

THE MEDITATIVE GARDENER

CONCLUSION

THIS BOOK DRAWS FROM THE structure of the Satipatthana Sutta, which concludes,

"…This is the direct path for the purification of beings, for the surmounting of sorrow and lamentation, for the disappearance of dukkha and discontent, for acquiring the true method, for the realization of Nibbana, namely, the four satipatthanas (the Four Foundations of Mindfulness)."

The Four Foundations of Mindfulness are the direct path to Awakening, and you have already begun the journey in your very own garden.

If the meditations and investigations in this book have led you to new insights, review them frequently in order to realize them in your life. You already know many things about how you could lead a wiser, healthier life, but insight alone does not usually transform us. Reviewing your insights often is like sprinkling your garden; eventually your insights penetrate to the roots. Then your life changes gradually, one moment at a time.

By now you have noticed that the Middle Way is not a linear path. It's more like a hologram with many entrances. One quality or practice, such as Mindfulness or Loving-Kindness, may help you find the doorway into your own meditative garden.

> May your garden be peaceful.
> May you be peaceful in your garden.
> May you abide in the well-being of your garden.
> May the merit of your gardening be shared by all beings everywhere.

GLOSSARY

bhante: Venerable Sir (a polite term used when addressing a Theravadin monk)

Bodhisattva: a person who has embarked on the path of enlightenment. In the Mahayana tradition, a Bodhisattva vows to postpone his or her own nirvana, out of compassion, in order to assist other beings.

Buddha: The name given to one who rediscovers for himself the liberating path of Dharma. The Buddha was born Siddhartha Gotama in north India in the sixth century BCE. A well-educated young man, he relinquished his family and his princely inheritance at age 29 to search for true freedom and an end to Suffering. After six years, he became an Awakened One, a Buddha.

citta: mind

dana: generosity

Dharma: the teachings of the Buddha

dukkha: suffering, stress, distress, dissatisfaction

karma: the law of cause and effect

metta (maitri): loving-kindness, loving-friendliness

nibbana (nirvana): liberation. Literally, an "unbinding" of the Mind.

panna: wisdom

samadhi: concentration

sangha: community

Satipatthana sutta: the discourse on the Four Foundations (or the Four Establishments) of Mindfulness—Body, Feelings, Mind and Mind Objects; the 10th sutta in the *Majjhima Nikaya* (MN10)

sila (shila): precepts or moral conduct, virtue, ethics

tonglen: sending and taking. Specifically taking in all that is harmful and sending out all that is positive and good.

upekkha: equanimity

vedana: feeling in the simple sense of pleasant, unpleasant, or neither-pleasant-nor-unpleasant

vipassana (vipashyana): insight

zabuton: a Japanese word for the large square mat underneath a zafu

zafu: a Japanese word for a meditation cushion (Think of "tofu" as a pillow of soy-bean curd.)

ACKNOWLEDGMENTS

A FOUR-WEEK RETREAT WITH AYYA Khema on videotape inspired this book. Perhaps because she had been an organic farmer in the 1960s and early 1970s before she was ordained, her Metta meditations are filled with gardening images which make my heart sing. Thanks to her Dharma heir, Bhante Nyanabodhi of Buddha Haus in Germany, for granting permission to use four of Ayya Khema's meditations in this book. Leigh Brasington, the senior American student of Ayya Khema, who has been teaching internationally since 1997, enlivened the Satipatthana sutta for me both by reciting suttas orally (with no notes) and by assigning one of the suggested meditations every week or so while I was on retreat.

What actually encouraged me to take pen to paper (and fingers to keyboard) however, was the assignment to do a Bodhisattva project while participating in the Community Dharma Leader training program at Spirit Rock Meditation Center in Woodacre, California, from 2005 to 2008.

Thanks to Andrew Olendzki, the executive director of the Barre Center for Buddhist Studies and a fine scholar, who opened my eyes to the Pali Canon.

Just as I was completing this manuscript, Claire Stanley, my longtime kalyana mitta and the guiding teacher of Vermont Insight Meditation Center, offered a study group on *Satipatthana* by Analayo. Analayo's combination of scholarship and practice refined my understanding of particular points.

Thanks to my critiquing group: Mary Mathias, Julie Chickering, Jayne Stout, Elizabeth Lewis, and our facilitator Jan Frazier (*When Fear Falls Away: The Story of a Sudden Awakening*) for their detailed comments and suggestions.

I feel extremely grateful to Susan Pollack, my editor, who trimmed the manuscript, tightened it up, and gave the sections a "through-story." Thanks also to David Carr for his editorial advice. Jenny Holan is the very good proof-reader who always comes through for me.

Thanks to the gardeners whom I quizzed about their gardening habits: Melissa Hays, Phyllis and Carol Young, Esther Falk, Perennial Swappers, and Sabrina Smith.

My morning sangha, Connie Woodberry and Lynn Levine, gave me unflinching feedback when I tried out these meditations on them; I thank them for their enduring support. I feel so grateful to be planted among such companions.

ENDNOTES

1. The little book *Gardener's Latin* by Bill Neal is the Rosetta Stone for deciphering Latin plant names.

2. Adapted from a guided meditation by the Venerable Ayya Khema. Before she was ordained as a nun at age 56, this German woman survived the Holocaust and had an organic farm in Australia in the 1970s.

3. For a deeper understanding of Loving-Kindness, read Sharon Salzberg's book, *Loving-Kindness: The Revolutionary Art of Happiness*.

4. The Satipatthana Sutta is in the *Middle Length Discourses* (MN 10).

5. For more ideas on walking meditation, read *The Long Road Turns to Joy: A Guide to Walking Meditation* by Thich Nhat Hanh.

6. If you have already received instructions for a Body Sweep from your meditation teacher, proceed with your usual practice. For a more complete version of the Body Scan, see *Full Catastrophe Living* by Jon Kabat-Zinn.

7. For more information on Craving, read *Hooked!*, edited by Stephanie Kaza.

8. *Radical Acceptance* by Tara Brach lays out the process of compassionately opening to difficult emotions.

9. Sylvia Boorstein has written a heart-warming book on the Paramis, *Pay Attention, For Goodness' Sake: Practicing the Perfections of the Heart—The Buddhist Path of Kindness*

10. Based on a meditation by Venerable Ayya Khema.

11. Downloading a Mindfulness Clock that bongs every hour helps me realize what time it is. It also offers me the opportunity to stop for a minute every hour and be Mindful of what I am doing http://www.Mindfulnessdc.org/Mindfulclock.html

12. Written by Reinhold Niebuhr

13. See Thich Nhat Hanh's statements of the Five Precepts, which he calls the Five Mindfulness Trainings, at www.plumvillage.org/MindfulnessTrainings/SMT.htm

14. To really get into this visualization, read the children's book *The Very Hungry Caterpillar* by Eric Carle.

15. The wooly bear or willyworm is the larva of the Isabella moth.

16. www.abirdsworld.com/Merchant2/merchant.mv?Screen=PROD&Store_Code=ABW&Product_Code=7755FFGp70&Category_Code=75

17. *The Herb Book* by John Lust, Bantam Books, 1974, p. 579.

18. www.ewg.org/reports/bodyburden/index.php

19. A Bodhisattva is a person who has embarked on the path to enlightenment. A Bodhisattva vows to postpone their own enlightenment in order to help others attain liberation.

20. Sylvia Boorstein in *Pay Attention for Goodness' Sake.*

21. James Joyce, *Dubliners,* "A Painful Case."

22. Larry Rosenberg has written an entire book on the five daily recollections entitled *Living in the Light of Death: On the Art of Being Truly Alive.*

23. Ruth Stout is the author of *How to Have a Green Thumb Without an Aching Back.* You can watch 92-year-old Ruth demonstrate her "no dig/no work" method of gardening on the DVD "Ruth Stout's Garden."

24. Chogyam Trungpa Rinpoche was one of the first Tibetan teachers in the United States. He began the Shambhala meditation centers and Naropa University. His students include Pema Chödrön and Allen Ginsberg.

25. Adapted from an Ayya Khema meditation.

26. A koan is a puzzling or paradoxical question asked in Zen Buddhism as an aid to meditation and in order to gain spiritual awakening.

27. *Weeds and What They Tell* by Ehrenfried E. Pfeiffer is published by Bio-Dynamic Farming and Gardening Association, Inc.

28. Lynn Levine is the co-author of *Mammal Tracks: Life-Size Tracking Guide* published by Heartwood Press.

29. To learn more about this woman who was a householder and a Buddhist master, read *Dipa Ma: The Life and Legacy of a Buddhist Master* by Amy Schmidt.

30. In the first stage of Awakening, a stream-enterer enters the stream which will lead to Nirvana. The three fetters—belief in a permanent self, attachment to rites and rituals, and Skeptical Doubt—are released.

    In the second state of Awakening, two fetters are weakened—Sense Desire and Ill Will—and the person becomes a once-returner. That is, they will be reborn one more time.

    In the third stage of Awakening, the fetters of Sense Desire and Ill Will are entirely removed and the person becomes a non-returner.

    In the fourth stage of Awakening, the remaining five fetters are released—attachment to form, attachment to formlessness, conceit, Restlessness, and Ignorance, and the person becomes an arahat, a person who has attained nirvana.

31. "Do unto others as you would have others do unto you." (Matthew 7:12), Christianity

    "This is the sum of duty: do not do to others what would cause pain if done to you." (Mahabharata 5:1517), Hinduism

"Not one of you truly believes until you wish for others what you wish for yourself." (Hadith), The Prophet Mohammed

"What is hateful to you, do not do to your neighbor. This is the whole Torah; all the rest is commentary. Go and learn it." Hillel, (Talmud, Shabbath 31a)

"I am a stranger to no one; and no one is a stranger to me. Indeed, I am a friend to all." Sikhism

"What you hate, do not do to anyone." (Tobit 4: 14-15).

"Do not impose on others what you do not desire others to impose upon you." (The Analects), Confucius

"Let no man do to another that which would be repugnant to himself." (Mahabharata, bk. 5, ch. 49, v. 57), Hinduism

"…What I condemn in another I will, if I may, avoid myself." (The Histories, bk. III, ch. 142), Herodotus.

"Hurt not others in ways you yourself would find hurtful." (Udana-Varga, 5.18)

"What things make you angry when you suffer them at the hands of others, do not you do to other people." Isocrates, the Greek orator:

"What you hate to suffer, do not do to anyone else." Philo, a Jewish philosopher

32. Think *Phila*delphia–the city of brotherly love, bibliophile–book lover, phytophile–plant lover, biophile–lover of nature. Philodendron "loves trees" because it clings to them in the rain forest.

33. Xenophobia means fear of foreigners. A xenophile is attracted to foreign styles, food or people.

34. *Mountains Beyond Mountains* by Tracy Kidder

35. *The Force of Kindness: change your life with love & compassion* by Sharon Salzburg focuses on healing yourself with compassion.
    The Compassion Box by Pema Chödrön contains a book, a CD and a set of 59 cards with pithy slogans.

36. A Bodhisattva is an enlightened being who postpones nirvana in order to help others.

37. Avalokitesvara is a Mahayana Bodhisattva who vowed to listen to the prayers of all beings in difficulty and postpone his own enlightenment.

38. *Tibetan Book of Living and Dying* by Sogyal Rinpoche, p. 205.

39. Memorial Day, July 4th, Veterans' Day. In Massachusetts, April 19th (now the third Monday in April), Patriots Day, celebrates Paul Revere's ride and "the shot heard 'round the world," fired in Concord on April 19, 1775.

40. *Radical Acceptance* by Tara Brach

PERMISSIONS

Thanks are extended to be following publishers and individuals for permission to reprint material copyrighted or controlled by them.

Beacon Press, Boston, for permission to reprint excerpts from *Time and the Garden: writings on a lifelong passion* Copyright © 2003 by Elisabeth Sheldon, pages 108, 117, and 149.

Copper Canyon Press, P.O. Box 271, Port Townshend, WA 98368-0271 for permission to reprint "The Shining Moment in the Now" from *While We've Still Got Feet: New Poems* Copyright © 2005 by David Budbill.

Perseus Press for permission to reprint an excerpt from "The Book of Time" from *Leaf and Cloud* Copyright © 2001 by Mary Oliver.

Random House for permission to reprint an excerpt from *The Education of a Gardener* Copyright © 1985 by Russell Page, page 63. *Also Pay Attention, For Goodness' Sake* Copyright © 2002 by Sylvia Boorstein, page 81.

W.W. Norton for permission to reprint excerpts from *The Wild Braid: A Poet Reflects on a Century in the Garden* by Stanley Kunitz with Genine Lentine. Copyright © 2005 by Stanley Kunitz and Genine Lentine, pages 3, 51, 54, 65.

Ajaan Lee Dhammadaro, *The Skill of Release*, 1995, translated by Thanissaro Bhikkhu.

Ajahn Chah, *Being Dharma: The Essence of the Buddha's Teachings*, Shambhala Publications, Inc., Copyright © 2005 by Paul Breiter, pages 79, 172-3.

Ayya Khema, *Visible Here and Now: The Buddha's Teachings on the Rewards of Spiritual Practice*, Shambhala Publications, Inc., 2001, pages 102-3, 146.

Bhikkhu Bodhi, *The Noble Eightfold Path: Way to the End of Suffering*, 2000, Pariyatti Publishing, pages 76, 78.

Bhikkhu Khantipalo, *Calm and Insight: A Buddhist Manual for Meditators*, 1987, Curzon Press, page 38.

Earth Prayers From Around the World edited by Elizabeth Roberts and Elias Amidon, 1991, p. 109.

Thich Nhat Hanh, *The Heart of The Buddha's Teaching: Transforming Suffering into Peace, Joy, and Liberation*, 1998, Parallax Press, pages 70, 71, 131, 186-7.

Thich Nhat Hanh, "The Nobility of Suffering," *Dharma, Color, and Culture: New Voices in Western Buddhism*, Parallax Press, page 62.

T Namaya for permission to reprint "one hundred flowers of peace."

Sangharakshita, *Living with Awareness: a Guide to the Satipaṭṭhāna Sutta*, Windhorse Publications, 2003, page148.

Sayadaw U Tejaniya, *Don't Look Down on the Defilements: They Will Laugh at You*, page 60.

Sharon Salzberg, *Loving-Kindness: The Revolutionary Art of Happiness*, Shambhala Publications, Inc., 1995, page 39.

All efforts have been made to contact copyright holders of material quoted in this book. However, if we have unwittingly infringed copyright in any way, we offer our sincere apologies and will be glad of the opportunity to make appropriate acknowledgment in future editions.